Mastering Algorithms: Solve Complex Problems with Ease

A Step-by-Step Guide to Algorithmic Thinking and Optimization

MIGUEL FARMER

RAFAEL SANDERS

Table of Content

TABLE OF CONTENTS

INTRODUCTION 7

Mastering Algorithms: Solve Complex Problems with Ease
.... 7

Why This Book? 7

What Will You Learn? 8

How Will You Benefit? 9

Who Is This Book For? 10

How to Use This Book 11

Conclusion 11

Chapter 1 13

Introduction to Algorithms and Problem Solving 13

    Summary of Chapter 1 20

Chapter 2 21

Basics of Algorithmic Thinking 21

    Summary 27

Chapter 3 29

Complexity and Big-O Notation 29

    Summary of Chapter 3 38

Chapter 4 39

Fundamental Data Structures 39

    Summary of Chapter 4 49

Chapter 5 51

Recursion: Solving Problems the Smart Way 51

Summary of Chapter 5 59

Chapter 6 61

Searching Algorithms 61

Summary of Chapter 6 69

Chapter 7 70

Sorting Algorithms 70

Summary of Chapter 7 84

Chapter 8 85

Divide and Conquer Algorithms 85

Summary of Chapter 8 93

Chapter 9 95

Greedy Algorithms 95

Summary of Chapter 9 102

Chapter 10 104

Dynamic Programming 104

Summary of Chapter 10 113

Chapter 11 115

Backtracking Algorithms 115

Summary of Chapter 11 125

Chapter 12 127

Graph Algorithms 127

Summary of Chapter 12 134

Chapter 13 135

Shortest Path Algorithms 135

Summary of Chapter 13 142

Chapter 14 144

Minimum Spanning Tree Algorithms 144

Summary of Chapter 14 150

Chapter 15 152

Network Flow Algorithms 152

Summary of Chapter 15 160

Chapter 16 162

String Matching and Text Processing 162

Summary of Chapter 16 173

Chapter 17 175

Advanced Data Structures 175

Chapter 18 188

Bit Manipulation 188

Summary of Chapter 18 196

Chapter 19 198

Computational Geometry Algorithms 198

Summary of Chapter 19 207

Chapter 20 209

Randomized Algorithms 209

Summary of Chapter 20 218

Chapter 21 219

Optimization Algorithms 219

Chapter 22 232

Approximation Algorithms 232

Summary of Chapter 22 241

Chapter 23 242

Parallel Algorithms 242

Summary of Chapter 23 250

Chapter 24 251

Machine Learning Algorithms 251

Chapter 25 262

Algorithm Optimization Techniques 262

    Summary of Chapter 25 270

Chapter 26 272

Debugging and Testing Algorithms 272

    Summary of Chapter 26 283

Chapter 27 284

Real-World Use Cases and Applications 284

    Summary of Chapter 27 292

INTRODUCTION

Mastering Algorithms: Solve Complex Problems with Ease

In today's fast-paced technological world, algorithms are the backbone of every innovation, from the simplest programs to the most complex artificial intelligence (AI) systems. The ability to design efficient, scalable, and optimized algorithms is crucial for problem-solving in fields like computer science, data analysis, machine learning, robotics, finance, and more. This book, **"Mastering Algorithms: Solve Complex Problems with Ease"**, is your guide to understanding the principles, techniques, and applications of algorithms, helping you sharpen your problem-solving skills and optimize your solutions for real-world scenarios.

Why This Book?

Whether you're a student just starting to explore the field of algorithms or an experienced programmer looking to refine your skills, this book offers something for everyone. You will learn the theory behind algorithms and gain practical experience through hands-on examples and exercises. The goal is to make the complex world of algorithms accessible to both beginners and experts, helping you master the fundamentals while exploring advanced topics in-depth.

In this book, we take a **problem-solving approach** to learning algorithms. Each chapter focuses on a different type of algorithm or a key aspect of algorithm design and optimization. You'll learn not only how to solve specific problems but also how to approach algorithmic thinking, which is vital for solving any computational problem.

What Will You Learn?

This book covers the most important topics in the field of algorithms, starting with the basics and gradually moving to more advanced techniques. Here's what you can expect to learn:

- **Foundational Algorithm Concepts**: You'll start by learning about algorithm analysis, time and space complexity, and how to evaluate the performance of algorithms.
- **Classic Algorithms**: We cover a broad spectrum of classic algorithms, including sorting, searching, dynamic programming, graph algorithms, divide-and-conquer, greedy algorithms, and more.
- **Optimization Techniques**: We delve into optimization algorithms, including parallel algorithms, approximation

algorithms, and those focused on enhancing both time and space efficiency.

- **Machine Learning Algorithms**: The book introduces you to the fundamental algorithms used in machine learning, such as linear regression, decision trees, and clustering techniques, and explores how they differ from traditional algorithms.

- **Real-World Applications**: With case studies from industries like **e-commerce**, **healthcare**, and **autonomous vehicles**, you will see how algorithms are used to solve complex real-world problems.

- **Testing and Debugging**: In addition to learning algorithm design, you will understand how to test and debug algorithms to ensure correctness and efficiency.

- **Future Trends**: The book explores cutting-edge trends in algorithm development, such as **quantum algorithms**, **AI algorithms**, and the role of algorithms in **big data** and **edge computing**.

How Will You Benefit?

By the end of this book, you will:

- **Master Algorithmic Thinking**: Gain the ability to break down complex problems and devise efficient algorithms to solve them.

- **Develop a Deep Understanding of Algorithm Design**: Learn how to create algorithms that are not only correct but also optimized for time and space efficiency.
- **Apply Algorithms to Real-World Problems**: You'll gain the skills to apply algorithms in real-world scenarios, from database optimization to AI-powered applications and more.
- **Learn Through Hands-On Exercises**: Each chapter includes practical examples and exercises, allowing you to implement algorithms and test them for correctness and efficiency.

Who Is This Book For?

This book is designed for:

- **Beginners**: If you are new to algorithms or programming, this book will guide you through the basics of algorithm design, optimization, and analysis in a clear and approachable manner.
- **Intermediate Programmers**: If you already have some experience with algorithms but want to expand your knowledge, you'll find deeper insights into advanced techniques like dynamic programming, graph algorithms, and parallel algorithms.
- **Experienced Developers**: Even if you're an experienced developer, the real-world case studies and optimization

techniques presented in this book will provide valuable insights into how algorithms are applied in industry and how to refine your coding practices.

How to Use This Book

This book is structured in a way that allows you to read through from start to finish or to jump to specific topics that interest you. If you're new to algorithms, we recommend reading the chapters sequentially to build a solid understanding. However, if you're already familiar with certain topics, you can focus on more advanced chapters such as **machine learning algorithms**, **parallel algorithms**, and **algorithm optimization**.

Each chapter begins with an introduction to the theory behind the algorithm, followed by practical examples and code snippets that demonstrate how to implement the algorithm. The exercises at the end of each chapter will help reinforce your learning and give you hands-on experience.

Conclusion

"Mastering Algorithms: Solve Complex Problems with Ease" is more than just a book about algorithms; it is a comprehensive guide that will help you develop a systematic approach to problem-solving. By the end of this book, you will not only understand how to design algorithms but also how to optimize them for efficiency, apply them to real-world problems, and stay ahead of emerging trends in algorithm development.

Let's dive into the world of algorithms and embark on a journey toward mastering the art of problem-solving in computer science!

CHAPTER 1

INTRODUCTION TO ALGORITHMS AND PROBLEM SOLVING

What is an Algorithm? Definition and Importance in Computing

An **algorithm** is a step-by-step procedure or set of rules designed to perform a specific task or solve a problem. In its simplest form, an algorithm takes some input, performs a series of steps, and produces an output. The idea is to break down a complex problem into smaller, manageable tasks that can be solved efficiently and effectively.

In computing, algorithms are the foundation of every software application and system. Whether you're building a website, designing a mobile app, or developing an artificial intelligence (AI) model, algorithms are at the heart of making the system function as expected. Algorithms help us make decisions, process data, find solutions, and optimize tasks in ways that are faster, more efficient, and scalable.

Key Characteristics of Algorithms:

13

- **Input**: The algorithm should take inputs that are clearly defined and structured.
- **Output**: The algorithm should produce an output based on the inputs.
- **Definiteness**: Each step of the algorithm must be clear and unambiguous.
- **Finiteness**: The algorithm must terminate after a finite number of steps.
- **Effectiveness**: The algorithm must solve the problem within a reasonable amount of time and resources.

Algorithms have a significant role in every aspect of computing, from managing user data to optimizing performance and ensuring security. **Understanding how to design and implement algorithms is critical to solving problems effectively**.

Real-World Examples of Algorithms

Algorithms are present in virtually every technology that we use today. Let's take a look at some **real-world examples** of algorithms:

1. **Search Engines (Google, Bing, etc.)**: Search engines rely on complex algorithms to rank and retrieve relevant information from millions (or billions) of webpages based on a search query. For example, when you type a search

term into Google, the algorithm evaluates multiple factors like page content, relevance, keywords, backlinks, and user behavior to return the most relevant results.

o **How it works**: A search algorithm processes vast amounts of data and ranks the results based on relevance. Google uses algorithms like **PageRank** to rank pages based on the number and quality of links pointing to them.

2. **Recommendation Systems (Netflix, Amazon, Spotify, etc.)**: Recommendation algorithms are designed to predict what a user might like based on their previous interactions, preferences, and behavior. Netflix suggests movies based on what you have watched in the past, and Amazon recommends products based on your browsing and purchase history.

o **How it works**: Collaborative filtering and content-based algorithms are used to make recommendations. These algorithms analyze data from multiple users and find patterns in their preferences to suggest products, movies, or music that match similar tastes.

3. **GPS Navigation Systems (Google Maps, Waze, etc.)**: GPS navigation systems use algorithms to determine the shortest or fastest route between two locations. The algorithms factor in real-time data, such as traffic, road closures, and accidents, to provide the most efficient path.

- o **How it works**: Algorithms like **Dijkstra's Algorithm** or *A Search** are used to find the optimal route. These algorithms take into account distance, traffic, and other road conditions to calculate the best route in real-time.

The Role of Algorithms in Solving Problems

Algorithms are essential for solving problems efficiently in computing. Problems, especially in large-scale systems, often involve vast amounts of data or require performing the same task multiple times. A good algorithm can make a huge difference in terms of **speed**, **accuracy**, and **resource utilization**.

For example, let's say you have a list of thousands of numbers, and you need to find the largest number. You could look at each number one by one, but an algorithm like **Quicksort** or **Merge Sort** can help you find that number much faster by reducing the time complexity.

Examples of Problem Solving with Algorithms:

- **Sorting Data**: Sorting is one of the most common problems in computer science, and there are many algorithms like **Bubble Sort**, **Merge Sort**, and **Quick Sort** to solve this problem efficiently.

- **Finding the Shortest Path**: Algorithms like **Dijkstra's Algorithm** or *A Search** can be used to find the shortest path between two points, whether in a road network or a graph.
- **Searching Data**: Searching algorithms like **Binary Search** allow you to find an item in a sorted list much faster than a linear search.

By using the right algorithm, you can improve the performance of your program, reduce the complexity of your problem, and handle much larger datasets.

Overview of Algorithmic Thinking and the Approach to Solving Complex Problems

Algorithmic thinking is the ability to approach problems systematically and break them down into smaller, solvable parts. This kind of thinking is essential for solving complex problems, whether you are working with data structures, building machine learning models, or optimizing your code.

The approach to solving problems algorithmically typically follows these steps:

1. **Problem Understanding**:

- o The first step is to understand the problem thoroughly. You need to identify what inputs are provided, what outputs are expected, and any constraints or conditions that must be met.
- o Example: If you are solving a route optimization problem, the input might include a map of roads, and the output would be the shortest path between two locations.

2. **Breaking Down the Problem**:
   - o Break the problem into smaller, manageable sub-problems. This step involves figuring out how you can divide the problem into smaller steps that can be solved individually.
   - o Example: In a graph traversal problem, you could break down the problem by identifying individual nodes and edges that need to be processed.

3. **Choosing the Right Approach**:
   - o Select an appropriate **algorithm** that fits the problem. Depending on the task, you might need a sorting algorithm, a searching algorithm, a dynamic programming solution, or a graph traversal technique.
   - o Example: For the shortest path problem, you might choose **Dijkstra's Algorithm** if all edges have non-negative weights.

4. **Designing the Algorithm**:

o Create a step-by-step procedure or set of instructions for solving the problem. This step will involve outlining the core logic and ensuring it efficiently handles the input and produces the correct output.

o Example: When solving a search problem, you would design a loop to iterate through the list and check for matching values.

5. **Optimizing the Solution**:

   o After designing a working solution, optimize the algorithm for efficiency. This could mean improving the algorithm's **time complexity** (how fast it runs) or **space complexity** (how much memory it uses).

   o Example: Instead of using a simple linear search, you might switch to **binary search** for faster lookups if the data is sorted.

6. **Testing and Refining**:

   o Finally, test your algorithm with various inputs and edge cases to ensure it works as expected. Refining the algorithm might involve fixing bugs, improving performance, or handling edge cases that weren't initially considered.

   o Example: For a sorting algorithm, test with arrays of varying sizes, empty arrays, and arrays with duplicate elements.

By approaching problems with **algorithmic thinking**, you learn how to tackle even the most complex problems methodically and effectively. This approach not only helps in solving problems in programming but also in real-life situations where problems can be broken down into smaller, solvable parts.

Summary of Chapter 1

In this chapter, we introduced the concept of **algorithms**, their importance in computing, and how they play a crucial role in solving problems across various domains. We explored real-world examples, such as search engines, recommendation systems, and GPS navigation, to illustrate how algorithms work in practice. We also discussed the significance of **algorithmic thinking** and the process of solving complex problems step-by-step, which is essential for both beginners and experts in the field of algorithm design.

As we move forward in the book, we will dive deeper into specific algorithms, optimization techniques, and real-world applications, giving you the tools to solve complex problems efficiently and effectively.

CHAPTER 2

BASICS OF ALGORITHMIC THINKING

Understanding How to Break Problems into Smaller Parts

One of the key skills in algorithmic thinking is the ability to break a large, complex problem into smaller, more manageable subproblems. This process of decomposition allows you to focus on one part of the problem at a time and ensures that each part can be solved independently and efficiently.

Why is problem decomposition important?

- **Simplification**: By breaking a problem into smaller parts, it becomes easier to focus on solving each part individually without getting overwhelmed by the complexity.
- **Parallelism**: Smaller problems can sometimes be solved simultaneously, improving overall efficiency.
- **Reusability**: Solving subproblems can create reusable components that can be applied to other problems in the future.
- **Manageability**: It allows you to clearly define steps and logic, reducing the chance of mistakes.

Example: Sorting a Deck of Cards Suppose you want to sort a deck of cards. The overall problem is to sort 52 cards, but if we break this down, we could:

1. Separate the problem into individual cards.
2. Identify which cards are in the wrong position.
3. Swap cards as needed until the deck is ordered.

This helps you focus on smaller steps (sorting individual cards) rather than trying to solve the entire problem all at once.

Importance of Logical Reasoning in Algorithm Design

Logical reasoning is the foundation of algorithmic thinking. It involves understanding how each step in the algorithm interacts with the data and how to achieve the desired outcome through logical steps. Without logical reasoning, algorithms can be inefficient or fail to produce the correct result.

Here's how logical reasoning helps:

1. **Clarity of Thought**: A well-thought-out algorithm minimizes errors and clarifies the relationships between data and operations.
2. **Correctness**: Logical reasoning ensures that every step leads to the intended solution without unnecessary complexity or mistakes.

3. **Efficiency**: By reasoning through the problem, you can optimize the algorithm and minimize unnecessary work, such as avoiding redundant calculations or operations.

4. **Edge Case Handling**: Logical reasoning helps you identify edge cases, such as handling empty inputs or maximum boundary conditions, which are often overlooked.

Example: Consider the problem of finding the largest number in an array. A logical approach would be:

- Start by assuming the first number is the largest.
- Compare each subsequent number to this largest value and update it if a larger number is found.
- After completing the comparison, the largest number will be the correct answer.

This approach is logical because it ensures that each comparison is relevant and helps to progressively build the solution.

Step-by-Step Approach: Input, Processing, Output

A fundamental aspect of algorithmic thinking is understanding the flow of an algorithm through three key stages: **input, processing, and output**. This structure provides a clear and systematic way to approach problems.

1. **Input**: The input is the data that the algorithm will operate on. This could be anything from a list of numbers to a complex data structure like a tree or graph.

2. **Processing**: This is the part of the algorithm where computations, comparisons, iterations, and other logical steps occur. The processing transforms the input into a useful result.

3. **Output**: The output is the result that the algorithm produces after processing the input. It could be a number, a string, or any other data structure depending on the problem.

Example: Sorting a Deck of Cards Using Basic Algorithms

Let's take the example of **sorting a deck of cards** using a **basic algorithm**, such as **Bubble Sort**. Here's how it fits into the input-processing-output structure:

- **Input**: The deck of cards, represented as a list of values. Each card has a rank (e.g., 2, 3, 4, ..., Ace) and a suit (e.g., hearts, diamonds, clubs, spades).

- **Processing**: In Bubble Sort, we compare adjacent cards in the list. If two cards are out of order, we swap them. This process is repeated until the entire list is sorted. The processing step involves iterating through the list multiple times to ensure the cards are in order.

- **Output**: The sorted deck of cards, with the cards arranged in increasing order of their rank and suit.

Here's a step-by-step breakdown of Bubble Sort:

1. Start with the first card and compare it with the next card.
2. If the first card is larger than the second, swap them.
3. Move to the next card and repeat the process until the end of the deck.
4. After the first pass, the largest card will have "bubbled up" to the end.
5. Repeat the process for the remaining cards, ignoring the last card (since it's already sorted).
6. Continue this process until no more swaps are needed, indicating that the deck is sorted.

This simple sorting algorithm processes the deck by repeatedly checking and swapping adjacent cards, ensuring the cards are sorted step by step.

Example: Sorting a Deck of Cards Using Basic Algorithms

Let's explore how **Bubble Sort** works by applying it to a deck of cards. For simplicity, let's assume the deck is represented as a list of integers, where each number corresponds to a card's rank. A deck with cards numbered 1 to 5 might look like this:

python

```
deck = [5, 3, 1, 4, 2]
```

We want to sort this deck in ascending order.

Bubble Sort Algorithm:

1. Compare the first element with the next element. If the first is larger, swap them.
2. Continue comparing and swapping adjacent elements until the end of the list.
3. After each pass, the largest element will be in the correct position, so we can exclude it from future passes.
4. Repeat this process until the list is sorted.

python

```
def bubble_sort(deck):
    n = len(deck)
    for i in range(n):
        # Last i elements are already in place
        for j in range(0, n-i-1):
            if deck[j] > deck[j+1]:
                deck[j], deck[j+1] = deck[j+1],
deck[j]   # Swap the cards
    return deck

deck = [5, 3, 1, 4, 2]
```

```
sorted_deck = bubble_sort(deck)
print(sorted_deck)
```

Output:

```
csharp
```

```
[1, 2, 3, 4, 5]
```

Step-by-Step Breakdown:

- First pass: The largest card, 5, "bubbles" to the end.
- Second pass: The second-largest card, 4, bubbles to its correct position.
- This process continues until the entire deck is sorted.

Bubble Sort is a **basic algorithm** that demonstrates how you can break down a problem (sorting a deck of cards) into smaller steps, process each comparison and swap, and produce the desired output.

Summary

In Chapter 2, we discussed the basics of **algorithmic thinking** and how breaking problems into smaller parts can simplify the process of finding solutions. We explored the importance of **logical reasoning** in designing algorithms and learned the basic approach of **input-processing-output**. By using the **Bubble Sort algorithm** as a practical example, we showed how an algorithm works step-by-step to solve a problem.

As you progress through the rest of the book, we will dive deeper into more advanced algorithms, focusing on optimizing solutions and applying them to real-world problems. Understanding the foundational principles of algorithmic thinking will serve as a solid base for tackling more complex challenges in algorithm design.

CHAPTER 3

COMPLEXITY AND BIG-O NOTATION

Understanding Time and Space Complexity

When analyzing an algorithm, we need to evaluate how **efficient** it is in terms of the resources it consumes. The two primary resources are **time** (how long the algorithm takes to run) and **space** (how much memory it uses). **Time complexity** and **space complexity** are used to describe the performance of an algorithm.

1. **Time Complexity**:
    o   Time complexity measures the amount of time an algorithm takes to complete as a function of the input size. It helps us understand how an algorithm's runtime grows as the input size increases.
    o   For example, if an algorithm takes twice as long to run with double the input size, we would expect its time complexity to be **O(n)** (linear time complexity).

2. **Space Complexity**:
    o   Space complexity measures the amount of memory an algorithm requires as a function of the

input size. This includes memory used by input data, temporary variables, and auxiliary data structures.

o For example, if an algorithm uses additional memory to store intermediate results, we need to account for that in the space complexity analysis.

These two metrics help determine how well an algorithm will perform with **large inputs** and how efficient it is in terms of computational resources.

Introduction to Big-O Notation for Evaluating Algorithm Efficiency

Big-O notation is a mathematical notation used to describe the upper bound of an algorithm's time or space complexity. It provides an upper limit on the growth of an algorithm's resource consumption as the input size increases.

In other words, Big-O notation tells us **how the performance of an algorithm scales** with the size of the input. It allows us to classify algorithms based on their **worst-case performance**.

Common Big-O Notations:

1. **O(1) - Constant Time**:
   o The algorithm's execution time remains constant regardless of the input size.

30

     o   Example: Accessing an element in an array by index.

python

```python
def get_element(arr, index):
    return arr[index]    #  O(1)    time
complexity
```

2. **O(log n) - Logarithmic Time**:
   - o The algorithm's execution time grows logarithmically as the input size increases. Algorithms that **divide** the problem in half at each step (like binary search) have this complexity.
   - o Example: Binary Search.

python

```python
def binary_search(arr, target):
    low, high = 0, len(arr) - 1
    while low <= high:
        mid = (low + high) // 2
        if arr[mid] == target:
            return mid
        elif arr[mid] < target:
            low = mid + 1
        else:
            high = mid - 1
    return -1  # O(log n) time complexity
```

31

3. **O(n) - Linear Time**:
   - o The algorithm's execution time grows directly with the input size.
   - o Example: Linear Search.

python

```python
def linear_search(arr, target):
    for i in range(len(arr)):
        if arr[i] == target:
            return i
    return -1 ' # O(n) time complexity
```

4. **O(n log n) - Linearithmic Time**:
   - o The execution time grows as the product of n and log n. This is typically the time complexity of more efficient sorting algorithms like **Merge Sort** or **Quick Sort**.
   - o Example: Merge Sort.

python

```python
def merge_sort(arr):
    if len(arr) <= 1:
        return arr
    mid = len(arr) // 2
    left = merge_sort(arr[:mid])
    right = merge_sort(arr[mid:])
    return merge(left, right)
```

```python
def merge(left, right):
    result = []
    i = j = 0
    while i < len(left) and j < len(right):
        if left[i] < right[j]:
            result.append(left[i])
            i += 1
        else:
            result.append(right[j])
            j += 1
    result.extend(left[i:])
    result.extend(right[j:])
    return result    # O(n log n) time
complexity
```

5. **O(n²) - Quadratic Time**:

   o The algorithm's execution time grows quadratically with the input size. This is common with algorithms that use nested loops.

   o Example: Bubble Sort.

python

```python
def bubble_sort(arr):
    n = len(arr)
    for i in range(n):
        for j in range(0, n - i - 1):
            if arr[j] > arr[j + 1]:
```

```
        arr[j], arr[j + 1] = arr[j
+ 1], arr[j]   # O(n²) time complexity
```

6. **O(2^n) - Exponential Time**:
   - ○ The execution time doubles with each additional input element. This type of complexity is often seen in algorithms that solve problems by brute force (e.g., generating all subsets or solving recursive problems).
   - ○ Example: Recursive Fibonacci.

python

```
def fibonacci(n):
    if n <= 1:
        return n
    return fibonacci(n - 1) + fibonacci(n
- 2)   # O(2^n) time complexity
```

7. **O(n!) - Factorial Time**:
   - ○ This is the worst-case scenario and often arises in problems that require generating all permutations of a set.
   - ○ Example: Solving the Traveling Salesman Problem (TSP) via brute force.

Real-World Examples of Algorithm Performance

Understanding **Big-O notation** helps you evaluate the real-world performance of algorithms, especially when dealing with large datasets or systems with limited computational resources. Here are a few examples:

1. **Searching for an Element in a List**:
   - If you're searching for an item in a sorted list, a **binary search** will perform in **O(log n)** time, making it much faster than a **linear search**, which has a time complexity of **O(n)**. For large datasets, the difference in performance becomes evident.

   Example:

   - **Binary Search (O(log n))**: Halves the search space with each comparison.
   - **Linear Search (O(n))**: Looks through each element one-by-one.

2. **Sorting a List**:
   - If you need to sort a list of numbers, **Merge Sort** or **Quick Sort** will generally perform better than simpler sorting algorithms like **Bubble Sort**.

Example:

- o **Merge Sort (O(n log n))**: Efficient for large datasets.
- o **Bubble Sort (O(n²))**: Inefficient for large datasets due to nested loops.

3. **Optimizing Database Queries**:
   - o **Indexing** in databases is a practical application of **O(log n)** complexity, which drastically reduces search times in large databases. Without indexing, searching for data in an unsorted database could take **O(n)** time, slowing down performance.

4. **Recommendation Systems**:
   - o Recommender systems, like those used by Netflix or Amazon, often use **O(n log n)** or **O(n)** algorithms to find the most relevant products or movies based on user preferences. As the data grows, choosing the right algorithm becomes more crucial to ensure the system remains responsive.

Why Big-O Matters in Large-Scale Systems

When building large-scale systems, Big-O notation becomes crucial because it allows you to:

- **Predict Performance**: Big-O provides a way to predict how the algorithm will behave as the input size increases. This is especially important when dealing with large datasets, real-time systems, or systems that require quick responses.

- **Optimize Resources**: As the system scales, optimizing algorithm performance can save both time and computational resources. For instance, switching from $O(n^2)$ to $O(n \log n)$ algorithms can significantly reduce processing time and improve user experience.

- **Handle Scalability**: Big-O notation helps identify potential bottlenecks. Algorithms that work fine with small datasets might slow down significantly with larger ones. By analyzing the time complexity, you can decide whether to optimize the existing algorithm or switch to a more efficient one.

- **Choose the Right Algorithm**: When building systems, Big-O helps you choose the most efficient algorithm for your use case. For example, for small datasets, a simple $O(n^2)$ algorithm like Bubble Sort might suffice, but for large datasets, an $O(n \log n)$ algorithm like Merge Sort is better.

In large-scale systems like social media platforms, e-commerce websites, or real-time data processing systems, Big-O notation guides engineers in building systems that can handle millions (or billions) of users without degrading performance.

Summary of Chapter 3

In this chapter, we explored the concepts of **time complexity** and **space complexity**, key factors in understanding how algorithms perform. We introduced **Big-O notation**, the standard way of evaluating and expressing the efficiency of algorithms. Big-O helps us classify algorithms based on their growth rates and understand how they perform as input sizes increase.

We discussed common Big-O notations and illustrated them with examples, from constant time (**O(1)**) to exponential time (**O(2^n)**). Real-world examples highlighted the importance of Big-O in everyday applications like searching, sorting, and recommendation systems. Finally, we explored why understanding Big-O is critical for **scalability**, **optimization**, and **resource management** in large-scale systems.

As we move forward, we'll continue to examine different algorithms and focus on how to optimize them for efficiency in solving real-world problems.

CHAPTER 4

FUNDAMENTAL DATA STRUCTURES

Introduction to Data Structures: Arrays, Linked Lists, Stacks, and Queues

Data structures are fundamental concepts in computer science and play a crucial role in how algorithms are designed and implemented. A **data structure** is a way of organizing and storing data so that it can be accessed and modified efficiently. In this chapter, we will explore the basic data structures that are commonly used in algorithm design: **arrays**, **linked lists**, **stacks**, and **queues**.

Each of these data structures has unique characteristics and serves different purposes in solving problems. Let's dive into the details:

1. Arrays

- An **array** is a collection of elements, all of the same type, stored in contiguous memory locations. Arrays allow you to access elements by their index in constant time **O(1)**.

   Characteristics of Arrays:

- o Fixed size: The size of an array is set when it is created and cannot be changed.
- o Contiguous memory allocation: All elements are stored in adjacent memory locations.
- o Accessing an element: Direct access to any element by index.

Example:

python

```
arr = [10, 20, 30, 40, 50]
print(arr[2])  # Access the third element,
output: 30
```

2. Linked Lists

- A **linked list** is a linear collection of elements, where each element (called a **node**) points to the next element. Unlike arrays, linked lists are dynamic, meaning they can grow or shrink in size.

Characteristics of Linked Lists:

- o Dynamic size: Linked lists can grow or shrink at runtime.
- o Non-contiguous memory allocation: Elements (nodes) can be stored anywhere in memory, and

40

each node contains a reference (or pointer) to the next node.

- o Sequential access: To access an element, you need to traverse the list from the beginning until you reach the desired node.

Example:

python

```python
class Node:
    def __init__(self, data):
        self.data = data
        self.next = None

head = Node(10)
second = Node(20)
head.next = second  # Pointing to the next node
print(head.next.data)  # Output: 20
```

3. Stacks

- A **stack** is a collection that follows the **LIFO (Last In, First Out)** principle, meaning the last element added to the stack is the first one to be removed.

Characteristics of Stacks:

41

- Operations: **push** (adding an element to the top) and **pop** (removing an element from the top).
- **Peek**: View the top element without removing it.
- Used for problems involving recursion, undo operations, and expression evaluation.

Example:

```
python

stack = []
stack.append(10)  # Push 10 onto the stack
stack.append(20)  # Push 20 onto the stack
print(stack.pop())  # Pop the top element,
output: 20
```

4. Queues

- A **queue** is a collection that follows the **FIFO (First In, First Out)** principle, meaning the first element added to the queue is the first one to be removed.

Characteristics of Queues:

- Operations: **enqueue** (adding an element to the rear) and **dequeue** (removing an element from the front).

o Used for tasks like scheduling, breadth-first search (BFS) in graph traversal, and message handling systems.

Example:

```python
python

from collections import deque

queue = deque()
queue.append(10)   # Enqueue 10
queue.append(20)   # Enqueue 20
print(queue.popleft())   # Dequeue the first
element, output: 10
```

How Data Structures Impact the Efficiency of Algorithms

The choice of **data structure** can significantly affect the **efficiency** of an algorithm. The operations that an algorithm needs to perform (such as insertion, deletion, searching, or sorting) will determine which data structure is most suitable for the task. Let's see how the choice of data structure can impact an algorithm's performance:

- **Arrays**: Accessing elements in an array is very fast (**O(1)**), but inserting or deleting elements can be slow (**O(n)**), especially when elements need to be shifted.

43

Arrays are useful when you need quick access to elements by index and when the size of the dataset is known beforehand.

- **Linked Lists**: Linked lists are dynamic and allow efficient **O(1)** insertions and deletions at the head or tail. However, accessing elements requires sequential traversal, which is **O(n)**. Linked lists are useful when you need frequent insertions or deletions, but random access is not as important.

- **Stacks**: Stacks are efficient for problems where the **LIFO** principle is applicable, such as recursion or depth-first search (DFS). Both **push** and **pop** operations take constant time **(O(1))**. However, random access to elements is not possible in a stack.

- **Queues**: Queues are ideal for problems that require processing elements in the order they arrive, such as breadth-first search (BFS) or handling tasks in scheduling systems. Both **enqueue** and **dequeue** operations are efficient **(O(1))**, but like stacks, random access to elements is not possible.

In summary, the **time complexity** of common operations and the **space complexity** of each data structure influence the overall efficiency of algorithms. The right data structure will lead to faster, more efficient algorithms, while the wrong one could lead to slower execution or increased resource consumption.

Real-World Examples of When to Use Each Data Structure

1. **Arrays**:
   - **Use case**: When you need to store data in a fixed-size collection and access elements by their index.
   - **Example**: Storing student grades, where you can quickly access a student's grade by their index (student ID).

2. **Linked Lists**:
   - **Use case**: When you frequently add and remove elements from the beginning or middle of a collection.
   - **Example**: Implementing a playlist where users can dynamically add or remove songs without rearranging the entire list.

3. **Stacks**:
   - **Use case**: When you need to track function calls, expressions, or undo operations in a last-in, first-out (LIFO) manner.
   - **Example**: Undo functionality in text editors, where the most recent action is undone first.

4. **Queues**:
   - **Use case**: When you need to process tasks in the order they arrive (first-in, first-out).

45

    o   **Example**: Managing print jobs in a printer queue or handling customer service requests in a call center.

Hands-On Exercise: Implementing and Using Basic Data Structures in Python

Now that we've introduced the fundamental data structures, let's go through an exercise where we will implement each of these data structures and explore how they can be used in practice.

1. Arrays

python

```python
# Implementing and using arrays (Python lists)
arr = [10, 20, 30, 40, 50]

# Accessing an element by index
print(arr[2])   # Output: 30

# Inserting an element at the end
arr.append(60)

# Deleting an element (by value)
arr.remove(20)

print(arr)   # Output: [10, 30, 40, 50, 60]
```

2. Linked Lists

python

```python
# Implementing a simple linked list in Python
class Node:
    def __init__(self, data):
        self.data = data
        self.next = None


class LinkedList:
    def __init__(self):
        self.head = None

    def append(self, data):
        new_node = Node(data)
        if not self.head:
            self.head = new_node
            return
        last = self.head
        while last.next:
            last = last.next
        last.next = new_node

    def display(self):
        current = self.head
        while current:
            print(current.data, end=" -> ")
            current = current.next
        print()
```

```
# Create a linked list and append elements
ll = LinkedList()
ll.append(10)
ll.append(20)
ll.append(30)

# Display the linked list
ll.display()  # Output: 10 -> 20 -> 30 ->
```

3. Stacks

python

```
# Implementing a stack using a Python list
stack = []

# Push elements onto the stack
stack.append(10)
stack.append(20)
stack.append(30)

# Pop an element from the stack
print(stack.pop())  # Output: 30

# Peek the top element
print(stack[-1])  # Output: 20
```

4. Queues

python

```
# Implementing a queue using collections.deque
```

```
from collections import deque

queue = deque()

# Enqueue elements
queue.append(10)
queue.append(20)
queue.append(30)

# Dequeue an element
print(queue.popleft())   # Output: 10

# Peek the front element
print(queue[0])   # Output: 20
```

Summary of Chapter 4

In this chapter, we introduced four **fundamental data structures**: arrays, linked lists, stacks, and queues. We explored their characteristics, use cases, and how they impact the efficiency of algorithms. We also provided hands-on exercises to help you understand how these data structures can be implemented and used in Python.

The choice of data structure is essential in algorithm design because it directly influences the efficiency of your solution. By mastering these basic data structures, you'll be able to tackle a wide range of problems in both coding interviews and real-world applications. In the next chapters, we'll continue building on this foundation as we dive deeper into more advanced data structures and algorithms.

CHAPTER 5

RECURSION: SOLVING PROBLEMS THE SMART WAY

What is Recursion? How Recursive Algorithms Work

Recursion is a programming technique where a function calls itself in order to solve a problem. The core idea behind recursion is to divide the problem into smaller, easier-to-solve subproblems, which are instances of the same problem.

A **recursive algorithm** works by breaking down a problem into simpler versions of itself, solving those smaller problems, and then combining the results to solve the original problem.

In a recursive function, two essential components are present:

1. **Recursive case**: This is where the function calls itself, usually with a smaller or simpler version of the original problem.
2. **Base case**: The base case defines the condition under which the function stops calling itself and begins to return values. Without a base case, recursion would continue indefinitely, causing a stack overflow.

Key Characteristics of Recursion:

- **Base case**: Prevents infinite recursion by providing a condition to stop the recursion.
- **Recursive case**: Defines the recursive call that breaks the problem into smaller subproblems.

Real-World Examples of Recursion

Let's look at a couple of **real-world examples** where recursion is commonly used: calculating the factorial of a number and performing binary search.

1. Calculating Factorial

The **factorial** of a number (denoted as **n!**) is the product of all positive integers from 1 to n. For example:

- $5! = 5 \times 4 \times 3 \times 2 \times 1 = 120$

The recursive definition of factorial is:

- **Base case**: The factorial of 0 is 1 (0! = 1).
- **Recursive case**: n! = n × (n-1)!

In this case, the recursive function breaks down the problem by multiplying n with the factorial of (n-1), and this continues until the base case is reached.

2. Binary Search

Binary Search is a search algorithm used to find the position of a target value within a **sorted array**. The idea is to repeatedly divide the array in half to narrow down the search space. Recursion is a natural fit for this algorithm.

- **Base case**: If the array has only one element, or if the target is found, we stop.
- **Recursive case**: If the target is smaller than the middle element, we recursively search the left half of the array; if the target is larger, we search the right half.

Binary search is much faster than linear search because it repeatedly halves the search space, making it a **logarithmic time algorithm ($O(\log n)$)**.

Identifying Base Cases and Recursive Cases

One of the most important aspects of designing a recursive algorithm is correctly identifying both the **base case** and the **recursive case**. Let's break down the steps involved in building a recursive function:

1. **Identify the base case(s):**

o The base case is the simplest form of the problem, which can be solved directly without recursion. It's essential for terminating the recursive calls.

o In most cases, the base case is when the input is small or has already been solved.

2. **Define the recursive case**:

o This is where the function calls itself with a simpler version of the problem. The recursive case should move the problem closer to the base case, ensuring that recursion eventually stops.

Let's look at an example using recursion to calculate the **factorial**.

Example 1: Factorial Using Recursion

The factorial function can be defined recursively as:

- **Base case**: If n = 0, return 1.
- **Recursive case**: Otherwise, return n * factorial(n-1).

python

```python
def factorial(n):
    # Base case
    if n == 0:
        return 1
    # Recursive case
    else:
        return n * factorial(n - 1)
```

```
# Example usage:
print(factorial(5))   # Output: 120
```

Explanation:

- When we call `factorial(5)`, the function will call `factorial(4)`, which calls `factorial(3)`, and so on, until it reaches `factorial(0)`, which returns 1. Then, the results are multiplied back together to give the final result (5 * 4 * 3 * 2 * 1 = 120).

Example 2: Binary Search Using Recursion

In binary search, the algorithm divides the search space in half with each recursive call. Let's assume the input array is already sorted.

- **Base case**: If the element is found, return its index. If the array is empty (low > high), return -1 to indicate the element is not found.
- **Recursive case**: If the target element is smaller than the middle element, recursively search the left half. If the target is larger, search the right half.

```python
def binary_search(arr, target, low, high):
    # Base case
```

```
    if low > high:
        return -1  # Element not found

    mid = (low + high) // 2

    if arr[mid] == target:
        return mid  # Element found
    elif arr[mid] > target:
        return binary_search(arr, target, low,
mid - 1)  # Search in the left half
    else:
        return binary_search(arr, target, mid +
1, high)  # Search in the right half

# Example usage:
arr = [1, 3, 5, 7, 9, 11, 13, 15, 17]
target = 7
print(binary_search(arr, target, 0, len(arr) -
1))  # Output: 3
```

Explanation:

- Initially, `low` is 0, and `high` is 8 (the last index). The middle element is `arr[4]` = 9. Since 7 is smaller than 9, the algorithm searches the left half, where `mid` is 2. This process continues until the element is found at index 3.

Exercise: Implementing Recursive Algorithms

Let's implement a few more recursive algorithms to solidify your understanding.

Exercise 1: Fibonacci Sequence

The **Fibonacci sequence** is defined as:

- **Base case**: Fibonacci(0) = 0, Fibonacci(1) = 1
- **Recursive case**: Fibonacci(n) = Fibonacci(n-1) + Fibonacci(n-2)

python

```python
def fibonacci(n):
    # Base cases
    if n == 0:
        return 0
    elif n == 1:
        return 1
    # Recursive case
    else:
        return fibonacci(n - 1) + fibonacci(n - 2)

# Example usage:
print(fibonacci(6))   # Output: 8
```

Explanation:

- `fibonacci(6)` will call `fibonacci(5)` and `fibonacci(4)`, and so on, until it reaches the base cases (0 and 1), where the recursion stops.

Exercise 2: Sum of Natural Numbers

Write a recursive function to calculate the sum of the first n natural numbers. The sum of the first n numbers is the sum of $1 + 2 + 3 + \ldots + n$.

- **Base case**: If `n == 0`, return 0.
- **Recursive case**: If `n > 0`, return `n + sum_of_numbers(n-1)`.

python

```python
def sum_of_numbers(n):
    # Base case
    if n == 0:
        return 0
    # Recursive case
    else:
        return n + sum_of_numbers(n - 1)

# Example usage:
print(sum_of_numbers(5))   # Output: 15 (1 + 2 +
3 + 4 + 5)
```

Explanation:

- When we call `sum_of_numbers(5)`, the function will call `sum_of_numbers(4)`, which calls `sum_of_numbers(3)`, and so on, until it reaches the base case `sum_of_numbers(0)` which returns 0. The recursion then adds the values together.

Summary of Chapter 5

In this chapter, we learned about **recursion** and how recursive algorithms work. We explored **real-world examples** of recursion, such as calculating the **factorial** of a number and performing **binary search**. We also emphasized the importance of identifying **base cases** and **recursive cases**, as these are essential for the correct functioning of recursive algorithms.

Through practical exercises, we implemented several recursive algorithms, including calculating the **Fibonacci sequence** and finding the **sum of natural numbers**. Recursion is a powerful tool in algorithmic thinking, and mastering it will help you solve complex problems efficiently.

As you continue through the book, we will build on this foundation to explore more advanced algorithms and techniques, including dynamic programming and backtracking, where recursion plays a central role in solving problems.

CHAPTER 6

SEARCHING ALGORITHMS

Linear Search vs. Binary Search

Searching algorithms are fundamental in computer science because they help locate specific elements in a collection of data. In this chapter, we'll explore two common searching algorithms: **linear search** and **binary search**. We'll also compare their performance in terms of **time complexity** and look at real-world examples of when each method is used.

1. Linear Search

Linear search is the most straightforward searching algorithm. It works by checking each element in a collection (like a list or array) one by one until it finds the target value or exhausts the entire collection.

Characteristics:

- **Unsorted data**: Linear search does not require the data to be sorted, making it flexible.
- **Time Complexity**: The time complexity of linear search is $O(n)$, where n is the number of elements in the collection. This means that in the worst case, the algorithm might need to check every single element.

61

Algorithm:

1. Start at the first element of the array.
2. Compare it to the target value.
3. If a match is found, return the index of the target.
4. If no match is found, continue to the next element.
5. If you reach the end of the array without finding the target, return -1 (not found).

Example: Linear Search

python

```python
def linear_search(arr, target):
    for i in range(len(arr)):
        if arr[i] == target:
            return i  # Target found at index i
    return -1  # Target not found

# Example usage:
arr = [5, 3, 8, 6, 7, 1]
target = 8
print(linear_search(arr, target))   # Output: 2
(Index of 8)
```

2. Binary Search

Binary search is a much more efficient searching algorithm, but it requires the data to be sorted beforehand. Binary search works by repeatedly dividing the search space in half, eliminating half of the remaining elements with each comparison. This makes binary search much faster than linear search on large datasets.

Characteristics:

- **Sorted data**: Binary search requires the input array to be sorted.
- **Time Complexity**: The time complexity of binary search is **O(log n)**, where **n** is the number of elements. This logarithmic growth makes binary search much more efficient than linear search for large datasets.

Algorithm:

1. Start with the entire sorted array.
2. Find the middle element and compare it to the target.
3. If the target is equal to the middle element, return its index.
4. If the target is smaller, repeat the search on the left half of the array.
5. If the target is larger, repeat the search on the right half of the array.
6. If the array is exhausted (low > high), return -1 (not found).

Example: Binary Search

python

```
def binary_search(arr, target):
    low = 0
    high = len(arr) - 1

    while low <= high:
        mid = (low + high) // 2
        if arr[mid] == target:
            return mid  # Target found at index
mid
        elif arr[mid] < target:
            low = mid + 1  # Search in the right
half
        else:
            high = mid - 1  # Search in the left
half
    return -1  # Target not found

# Example usage:
arr = [1, 3, 5, 6, 7, 8]
target = 6
print(binary_search(arr, target))  # Output: 3
(Index of 6)
```

Comparison of Linear Search and Binary Search

Algorithm	Time Complexity	Space Complexity	When to Use
Linear Search	O(n)	O(1)	Use when data is unsorted or when

Algorithm	Time Complexity	Space Complexity	When to Use
			searching in small datasets.
Binary Search	O(log n)	O(1)	Use when the data is sorted or when you need a more efficient search in large datasets.

- **Linear Search** is simpler and more flexible because it doesn't require sorted data. However, it can be slower for large datasets because it must check every element.
- **Binary Search** is faster than linear search but requires sorted data. For large datasets, binary search can significantly reduce the search time compared to linear search.

Real-World Example: Searching in Databases or Arrays

In real-world applications, searching algorithms are frequently used in databases and large data sets. Let's take a closer look at how searching plays a role in common applications.

1. **Database Search**:

- o **Linear Search**: Used in smaller, unsorted data or when data cannot be pre-sorted due to specific constraints.
- o **Binary Search**: Often used in indexed databases where data is sorted. For example, searching for a specific record in a large database using a binary search index drastically improves performance.

2. **Searching in Arrays**:
   - o In smaller arrays, **linear search** might be sufficient. However, for large sorted arrays, **binary search** is preferred because of its logarithmic time complexity.

3. **Real-Time Systems**:
   - o In real-time systems, such as those used for trading algorithms or stock market analysis, quick searching and decision-making is crucial. A sorted data structure with binary search enables quick and efficient lookups.

Exercise: Implementing Linear and Binary Search Algorithms

In this exercise, we will implement both **linear search** and **binary search** algorithms in Python.

Linear Search Exercise:

1. Create a list of integers.
2. Implement a function to search for a target value in the list using linear search.
3. Test the function with different target values.

python

```python
def linear_search(arr, target):
    for i in range(len(arr)):
        if arr[i] == target:
            return i  # Target found at index i
    return -1  # Target not found


# Example usage:
arr = [45, 67, 23, 89, 12, 56]
target = 23
result = linear_search(arr, target)

if result != -1:
    print(f"Target found at index {result}")
else:
    print("Target not found")
```

Binary Search Exercise:

1. Create a sorted list of integers.
2. Implement a function to search for a target value using binary search.

3. Test the function with different target values.

python

```python
def binary_search(arr, target):
    low = 0
    high = len(arr) - 1

    while low <= high:
        mid = (low + high) // 2
        if arr[mid] == target:
            return mid   # Target found at index mid
        elif arr[mid] < target:
            low = mid + 1   # Search in the right half
        else:
            high = mid - 1   # Search in the left half
    return -1   # Target not found

# Example usage:
arr = [1, 3, 5, 6, 7, 8, 10]
target = 6
result = binary_search(arr, target)

if result != -1:
    print(f"Target found at index {result}")
else:
    print("Target not found")
```

68

Summary of Chapter 6

In this chapter, we explored two common **searching algorithms**: **linear search** and **binary search**. We learned how linear search works by checking each element one-by-one, making it a good choice for unsorted data, but less efficient for large datasets. On the other hand, binary search is much faster (with **O(log n)** time complexity) but requires sorted data to function efficiently.

We also looked at real-world applications of these algorithms, such as searching in databases and arrays, and compared their performance in different use cases.

Through hands-on exercises, we implemented both linear and binary search algorithms, reinforcing the concepts and preparing you for more advanced algorithmic challenges. In the following chapters, we will explore more advanced algorithms and data structures to solve more complex problems efficiently.

CHAPTER 7

SORTING ALGORITHMS

Understanding Basic Sorting Algorithms: Bubble Sort, Insertion Sort, Selection Sort

Sorting algorithms are a fundamental concept in computer science. They arrange elements of a collection (such as an array or list) in a specific order, typically in ascending or descending order. Sorting is often one of the first problems tackled when learning algorithms, and understanding the most common sorting methods is essential.

Let's start by reviewing three **basic sorting algorithms**: **Bubble Sort**, **Insertion Sort**, and **Selection Sort**.

1. Bubble Sort

Bubble Sort is one of the simplest sorting algorithms. It works by repeatedly stepping through the list, comparing adjacent elements, and swapping them if they are in the wrong order. This process is repeated until the list is sorted.

- **Time Complexity**: $O(n^2)$ in the worst and average cases (due to nested loops).
- **Space Complexity**: $O(1)$ (in-place sorting).

70

Algorithm:

1. Start at the first element and compare it with the next.
2. If the first element is larger than the second, swap them.
3. Continue this process until the entire list is sorted.

Example:

python

```python
def bubble_sort(arr):
    n = len(arr)
    for i in range(n):
        for j in range(0, n-i-1):
            if arr[j] > arr[j+1]:
                arr[j], arr[j+1] = arr[j+1],
arr[j]  # Swap elements
    return arr


# Example usage:
arr = [64, 34, 25, 12, 22, 11, 90]
print(bubble_sort(arr))   # Output: [11, 12, 22,
25, 34, 64, 90]
```

2. Insertion Sort

Insertion Sort works similarly to how we might sort playing cards in our hands. It takes elements from the unsorted portion of the list and inserts them into their correct position in the sorted portion.

- **Time Complexity**: $O(n^2)$ in the worst case (when the list is reversed), but **O(n)** in the best case (when the list is already sorted).
- **Space Complexity**: **O(1)** (in-place sorting).

Algorithm:

1. Start with the second element (since the first element is trivially sorted).
2. Compare it to the first element. If it's smaller, move the first element to the right, and insert the second element in the correct position.
3. Repeat for each subsequent element, inserting it into the correct position relative to the previously sorted elements.

Example:

python

```python
def insertion_sort(arr):
    for i in range(1, len(arr)):
        key = arr[i]
        j = i - 1
        while j >= 0 and arr[j] > key:
            arr[j + 1] = arr[j]
            j -= 1
        arr[j + 1] = key
    return arr
```

```
# Example usage:
arr = [64, 34, 25, 12, 22, 11, 90]
print(insertion_sort(arr))    # Output: [11, 12,
22, 25, 34, 64, 90]
```

3. Selection Sort

Selection Sort works by repeatedly finding the smallest (or largest) element from the unsorted portion of the list and swapping it with the first unsorted element.

- **Time Complexity: O(n²)** due to the nested loops (one loop to select the smallest element and another to traverse the remaining unsorted elements).
- **Space Complexity: O(1)** (in-place sorting).

Algorithm:

1. Start by looking at the first element.
2. Find the smallest element in the unsorted portion of the list.
3. Swap the smallest element with the first unsorted element.
4. Repeat until the entire list is sorted.

Example:

python

```
def selection_sort(arr):
    n = len(arr)
```

73

```
for i in range(n):
    min_index = i
    for j in range(i+1, n):
        if arr[j] < arr[min_index]:
            min_index = j
    arr[i], arr[min_index] = arr[min_index],
arr[i]
    return arr

# Example usage:
arr = [64, 34, 25, 12, 22, 11, 90]
print(selection_sort(arr))   # Output: [11, 12,
22, 25, 34, 64, 90]
```

More Advanced Sorting Algorithms: Merge Sort, Quick Sort, Heap Sort

While the basic sorting algorithms are useful for small datasets, they are inefficient for larger datasets. More advanced sorting algorithms, such as **Merge Sort**, **Quick Sort**, and **Heap Sort**, are generally faster and more efficient.

1. Merge Sort

Merge Sort is a **divide-and-conquer** algorithm that divides the input list into two halves, recursively sorts each half, and then merges the sorted halves back together.

- **Time Complexity**: **O(n log n)** in the worst, average, and best cases.
- **Space Complexity**: **O(n)** (requires extra space for the temporary arrays used in the merge step).

Algorithm:

1. Split the array into two halves.
2. Recursively sort each half.
3. Merge the two sorted halves back together.

Example:

python

```python
def merge_sort(arr):
    if len(arr) > 1:
        mid = len(arr) // 2  # Find the middle
        left_half = arr[:mid]
        right_half = arr[mid:]

        merge_sort(left_half)      #  Recursively
sort the left half
        merge_sort(right_half)     #  Recursively
sort the right half

        i = j = k = 0

        # Merge the sorted halves
```

```
        while  i  <  len(left_half)  and  j  <
len(right_half):
            if left_half[i] < right_half[j]:
                arr[k] = left_half[i]
                i += 1
            else:
                arr[k] = right_half[j]
                j += 1
            k += 1

        # any remaining elements
        while i < len(left_half):
            arr[k] = left_half[i]
            i += 1
            k += 1
        while j < len(right_half):
            arr[k] = right_half[j]
            j += 1
            k += 1
    return arr


# Example usage:
arr = [64, 34, 25, 12, 22, 11, 90]
print(merge_sort(arr))   # Output: [11, 12, 22,
25, 34, 64, 90]
```

2. Quick Sort

Quick Sort is another **divide-and-conquer** algorithm that selects a "pivot" element and partitions the array into two sub-arrays (one with elements smaller than the pivot, and one with elements larger than the pivot). It then recursively sorts the sub-arrays.

- **Time Complexity**: **O(n log n)** on average, but **O(n²)** in the worst case (when the pivot is poorly chosen).
- **Space Complexity**: **O(log n)** (in-place sorting).

Algorithm:

1. Choose a pivot element.
2. Partition the array into two sub-arrays: elements less than the pivot and elements greater than the pivot.
3. Recursively sort the sub-arrays.

Example:

python

```
def quick_sort(arr):
    if len(arr) <= 1:
        return arr
    pivot = arr[len(arr) // 2]   # Choose the
middle element as the pivot
    left = [x for x in arr if x < pivot]
    middle = [x for x in arr if x == pivot]
    right = [x for x in arr if x > pivot]
    return  quick_sort(left)  +  middle  +
quick_sort(right)
```

```
# Example usage:
arr = [64, 34, 25, 12, 22, 11, 90]
print(quick_sort(arr))   # Output: [11, 12, 22,
25, 34, 64, 90]
```

3. Heap Sort

Heap Sort is a comparison-based sorting algorithm that uses a **heap** data structure (typically a binary heap) to sort elements. It first builds a max-heap and repeatedly extracts the maximum element, placing it at the end of the list.

- **Time Complexity**: **O(n log n)** in the worst, average, and best cases.
- **Space Complexity**: **O(1)** (in-place sorting).

Algorithm:

1. Build a max-heap from the input data.
2. Swap the root of the heap (the maximum element) with the last element.
3. Re-heapify the heap and repeat the process until the heap is empty.

Example:

python

```
def heapify(arr, n, i):
    largest = i
```

78

```python
    left = 2 * i + 1
    right = 2 * i + 2

    if left < n and arr[left] > arr[largest]:
        largest = left
    if right < n and arr[right] > arr[largest]:
        largest = right

    if largest != i:
        arr[i], arr[largest] = arr[largest], arr[i]
        heapify(arr, n, largest)

def heap_sort(arr):
    n = len(arr)

    # Build a max-heap
    for i in range(n // 2 - 1, -1, -1):
        heapify(arr, n, i)

    # Extract elements from the heap one by one
    for i in range(n-1, 0, -1):
        arr[i], arr[0] = arr[0], arr[i]   # Swap
        heapify(arr, i, 0)     # Re-heapify the reduced heap

    return arr

# Example usage:
```

```
arr = [64, 34, 25, 12, 22, 11, 90]
print(heap_sort(arr))   # Output: [11, 12, 22, 25,
34, 64, 90]
```

When to Use Each Sorting Algorithm Based on Input Size and Characteristics

- **Bubble Sort**:
    - o Best for small datasets or when simplicity is more important than performance.
    - o Inefficient for large datasets due to its **O(n²)** time complexity.
- **Insertion Sort**:
    - o Efficient for small datasets or nearly sorted data.
    - o Time complexity is **O(n)** when the data is already sorted or nearly sorted.
- **Selection Sort**:
    - o Similar to Bubble Sort and not generally efficient for large datasets.
    - o Useful when memory is limited, as it operates in-place with **O(1)** space complexity.
- **Merge Sort**:
    - o Preferred for large datasets where stability is required (e.g., sorting objects with multiple attributes).

- o **O(n log n)** time complexity makes it more efficient than **O(n²)** algorithms.
- **Quick Sort**:
  - o One of the fastest general-purpose sorting algorithms.
  - o Works well with large datasets, but the worst-case performance is **O(n²)**, which can be avoided by using a good pivot selection method.
- **Heap Sort**:
  - o Efficient for large datasets and when memory usage is critical (in-place sorting).
  - o **O(n log n)** time complexity makes it a good choice for situations where you don't need the stability of Merge Sort.

Real-World Example: Sorting Data for Analytics or Display

Sorting algorithms are widely used in real-world applications, such as data analysis, databases, and user interfaces.

1. **Data Analytics**:
   - o When analyzing large datasets (e.g., sorting sales data or search logs), **Merge Sort** and **Quick Sort** are often used because of their efficiency in handling large amounts of data.
2. **User Interface**:

o Sorting is frequently used in user interfaces to display lists of items, such as sorting emails by date, displaying product recommendations, or ranking search results.

3. **Databases**:

o Databases often use sorting algorithms to organize records before performing operations like searching, filtering, or displaying the data to users.

Exercise: Implementing Sorting Algorithms in Code

In this exercise, you will implement **Bubble Sort**, **Insertion Sort**, and **Selection Sort** and compare their performance using a sample dataset.

python

```python
# Implementing Bubble Sort
def bubble_sort(arr):
    n = len(arr)
    for i in range(n):
        for j in range(0, n-i-1):
            if arr[j] > arr[j+1]:
                arr[j], arr[j+1] = arr[j+1],
arr[j]
    return arr
```

```python
# Implementing Insertion Sort
def insertion_sort(arr):
    for i in range(1, len(arr)):
        key = arr[i]
        j = i - 1
        while j >= 0 and arr[j] > key:
            arr[j + 1] = arr[j]
            j -= 1
        arr[j + 1] = key
    return arr


# Implementing Selection Sort
def selection_sort(arr):
    n = len(arr)
    for i in range(n):
        min_index = i
        for j in range(i + 1, n):
            if arr[j] < arr[min_index]:
                min_index = j
        arr[i], arr[min_index] = arr[min_index], arr[i]
    return arr


# Example usage
arr = [64, 34, 25, 12, 22, 11, 90]
print("Bubble Sort:", bubble_sort(arr.()))
print("Insertion Sort:", insertion_sort(arr.()))
print("Selection Sort:", selection_sort(arr.()))
```

Summary of Chapter 7

In this chapter, we explored various **sorting algorithms**: **Bubble Sort**, **Insertion Sort**, and **Selection Sort**, as well as more advanced algorithms like **Merge Sort**, **Quick Sort**, and **Heap Sort**. We compared the time complexity and use cases of each algorithm, helping you understand when to apply each one based on input size and performance requirements.

We also worked through practical exercises to implement these sorting algorithms and compared their results. Sorting algorithms are a fundamental part of algorithm design and data processing, and mastering them will help you tackle a wide range of problems in computer science and software development.

CHAPTER 8

DIVIDE AND CONQUER ALGORITHMS

The Concept of Breaking a Problem into Smaller Subproblems

Divide and Conquer is a powerful algorithmic strategy used to solve problems by breaking them down into smaller, more manageable subproblems. The key idea is to divide the original problem into smaller, similar subproblems, solve these subproblems recursively, and then combine the solutions to form the final answer.

This technique is particularly useful because it allows us to handle complex problems in an organized manner, breaking down the complexity and making the problem easier to manage.

Steps in Divide and Conquer:

1. **Divide**: Break the problem into smaller subproblems. These subproblems should be easier to solve independently.

2. **Conquer**: Solve each subproblem recursively. If the subproblem is small enough, solve it directly (this is often called the **base case**).

3. **Combine**: Combine the results of the subproblems to form a solution to the original problem.

Examples of Divide and Conquer Algorithms: Merge Sort and Quick Sort

The most common examples of **divide and conquer** algorithms are **Merge Sort** and **Quick Sort**. Both algorithms use recursion to divide the problem into smaller parts and then combine the results.

1. Merge Sort

Merge Sort is a **divide and conquer** algorithm that works by dividing the array into two halves, sorting each half recursively, and then merging the two sorted halves into a single sorted array.

- **Time Complexity**: **O(n log n)** in the worst, average, and best cases.
- **Space Complexity**: **O(n)** (due to the need for temporary arrays during the merge process).

Steps in Merge Sort:

1. Divide the array into two halves.
2. Recursively sort both halves.
3. Merge the sorted halves.

```python
python

def merge_sort(arr):
    if len(arr) > 1:
        mid = len(arr) // 2   # Find the middle point
        left_half = arr[:mid]
        right_half = arr[mid:]

        merge_sort(left_half)    # Recursively sort the left half
        merge_sort(right_half)    # Recursively sort the right half

        i = j = k = 0

        # Merge the sorted halves
        while i < len(left_half) and j < len(right_half):
            if left_half[i] < right_half[j]:
                arr[k] = left_half[i]
                i += 1
            else:
                arr[k] = right_half[j]
                j += 1
            k += 1

        # any remaining elements
        while i < len(left_half):
```

```
        arr[k] = left_half[i]
        i += 1
        k += 1
    while j < len(right_half):
        arr[k] = right_half[j]
        j += 1
        k += 1


    return arr


# Example usage:
arr = [64, 34, 25, 12, 22, 11, 90]
print(merge_sort(arr))   # Output: [11, 12, 22,
25, 34, 64, 90]
```

2. Quick Sort

Quick Sort is another **divide and conquer** algorithm that works by selecting a "pivot" element from the array and partitioning the other elements into two sub-arrays, according to whether they are less than or greater than the pivot. The sub-arrays are then sorted recursively.

- **Time Complexity**: **O(n log n)** on average, but **O(n²)** in the worst case (when the pivot is poorly chosen).
- **Space Complexity**: **O(log n)** (in-place sorting).

Steps in Quick Sort:

1. Choose a pivot element.

2. Partition the array into two sub-arrays: elements less than the pivot and elements greater than the pivot.
3. Recursively sort the two sub-arrays.

python

```python
def quick_sort(arr):
    if len(arr) <= 1:
        return arr
    pivot = arr[len(arr) // 2]    # Choose the
middle element as the pivot
    left = [x for x in arr if x < pivot]
    middle = [x for x in arr if x == pivot]
    right = [x for x in arr if x > pivot]
    return   quick_sort(left)   +   middle   +
quick_sort(right)

# Example usage:
arr = [64, 34, 25, 12, 22, 11, 90]
print(quick_sort(arr))    # Output: [11, 12, 22,
25, 34, 64, 90]
```

Recursion in Divide and Conquer Strategies

Recursion is the backbone of the divide and conquer strategy. By applying recursion, the problem is divided into smaller subproblems that are easier to solve. The recursive calls continue breaking down the problem until the base case is reached, at which point the solution can be combined and returned.

In both **Merge Sort** and **Quick Sort**, recursion allows us to solve smaller subproblems (sorting smaller arrays) and then combine the results to solve the larger problem (sorting the entire array).

For example:

- **Merge Sort** recursively splits the array until each sub-array contains one element, which is trivially sorted, and then merges them back together.
- **Quick Sort** recursively partitions the array, narrowing down the search space until the entire array is sorted.

The recursive nature of divide and conquer algorithms leads to cleaner code and helps break down large, complex problems into smaller, more manageable pieces.

Real-World Example: Solving Complex Mathematical Problems or Algorithms in Computer Vision

Divide and Conquer is not limited to sorting. It is widely used in various fields like **computer vision**, **mathematics**, and **parallel processing**.

Example in Computer Vision:

- In **image processing**, large images are divided into smaller tiles or blocks for parallel processing. Each block is processed independently (e.g., applying filters, detecting edges), and then the results are combined to process the entire image. This is a typical application of **divide and conquer**.

Example in Mathematical Problems:

- **Multiplying large numbers**: One of the well-known applications of divide and conquer is **Karatsuba multiplication**, an algorithm used to multiply large numbers. It divides the numbers into smaller parts, multiplies them recursively, and combines the results, reducing the time complexity from $O(n^2)$ to $O(n^{\wedge}\log_2(3))$.

In both these fields, **divide and conquer** algorithms help improve the efficiency of the solution by reducing the problem size with each recursive step.

Exercise: Implementing a Divide-and-Conquer Sorting Algorithm

Let's implement a **Merge Sort** algorithm as part of this exercise. In this case, we'll work through the steps of the algorithm and explore how dividing the array into smaller sub-arrays leads to efficient sorting.

python

```python
def merge_sort(arr):
    # Base case: If the array has one element, it
is already sorted
    if len(arr) > 1:
        # Divide the array into two halves
        mid = len(arr) // 2
        left_half = arr[:mid]
        right_half = arr[mid:]

        # Recursively sort both halves
        merge_sort(left_half)
        merge_sort(right_half)

        i = j = k = 0

        # Merge the sorted halves
        while  i  <  len(left_half)  and  j  <
len(right_half):
            if left_half[i] < right_half[j]:
                arr[k] = left_half[i]
                i += 1
            else:
                arr[k] = right_half[j]
                j += 1
```

```
        k += 1

    #  any remaining elements
    while i < len(left_half):
        arr[k] = left_half[i]
        i += 1
        k += 1
    while j < len(right_half):
        arr[k] = right_half[j]
        j += 1
        k += 1

    return arr

# Example usage:
arr = [64, 34, 25, 12, 22, 11, 90]
print(merge_sort(arr))   # Output: [11, 12, 22,
25, 34, 64, 90]
```

Summary of Chapter 8

In this chapter, we explored **divide and conquer algorithms** and learned how breaking a large problem into smaller subproblems can lead to more efficient solutions. We discussed **Merge Sort** and **Quick Sort**, two common divide and conquer algorithms, and analyzed how recursion plays a key role in solving the subproblems.

We also looked at real-world applications of divide and conquer in fields like **computer vision** and **mathematics**, where this technique is used to improve efficiency and scalability.

Through the **hands-on exercise**, we implemented a divide-and-conquer sorting algorithm (Merge Sort) and observed how the recursive approach efficiently divides the problem, solves the subproblems, and combines the results.

In the next chapters, we will dive deeper into other algorithms that benefit from divide and conquer strategies and explore advanced topics like **dynamic programming** and **graph algorithms**.

CHAPTER 9

GREEDY ALGORITHMS

The Greedy Approach: Making the Best Local Choice at Each Step

Greedy algorithms are a class of algorithms that make the best possible choice at each step with the hope of finding the global optimum. The idea is to solve the problem by iteratively choosing the best option available at the current moment, without reconsidering previous choices. This approach often works well for certain types of problems, particularly when making the local optimal choice leads to the global optimal solution.

However, **greedy algorithms** are not guaranteed to work for all problems, and sometimes they can result in suboptimal solutions. They are efficient and easy to implement, but their applicability depends on the problem's structure.

Key Characteristics of Greedy Algorithms:

1. **Greedy Choice Property**: The optimal solution can be constructed by choosing the best option at each step.
2. **Optimal Substructure**: The problem can be broken down into smaller subproblems, and the optimal solution to the overall problem can be constructed from optimal solutions to subproblems.

Greedy algorithms typically work when the problem exhibits **optimal substructure** and **greedy choice property**.

Examples: Activity Selection, Coin Change Problem

Let's look at two classic problems where greedy algorithms are commonly used: **Activity Selection** and the **Coin Change Problem**.

1. Activity Selection Problem

The **Activity Selection Problem** involves selecting the maximum number of activities that can be performed in a given time period, where each activity has a start time and a finish time. The goal is to choose the maximum number of non-overlapping activities.

- **Greedy Approach**: Sort the activities by their finish times, and select the first activity that finishes. Then, select the next activity that starts after the previously selected activity finishes, and so on.

Algorithm:

1. Sort the activities based on their finish times.
2. Select the first activity.
3. For each subsequent activity, if its start time is after the finish time of the previously selected activity, select it.

python

```python
def activity_selection(activities):
    # Sort activities by finish time
    activities.sort(key=lambda x: x[1])

    selected_activities = []
    last_finish_time = -1

    for activity in activities:
        start, finish = activity
        if start >= last_finish_time:

selected_activities.append(activity)
            last_finish_time = finish

    return selected_activities

# Example usage:
activities = [(1, 4), (3, 5), (0, 6), (5, 7), (3,
8), (8, 9)]
print(activity_selection(activities))  # Output:
[(1, 4), (5, 7), (8, 9)]
```

2. Coin Change Problem

The **Coin Change Problem** involves making a certain amount of change using the least number of coins from a given set of denominations. The greedy approach works optimally when the coin denominations are **multiples** of each other.

- **Greedy Approach**: Start with the largest coin denomination, use as many of that coin as possible, then move to the next largest coin, and continue until the total amount is reached.

Algorithm:

1. Sort the coin denominations in descending order.
2. Start with the largest denomination and use as many of that denomination as possible.
3. Move to the next denomination and repeat until the total is reached.

python

```python
def coin_change(coins, amount):
    coins.sort(reverse=True)    # Sort coins in
descending order
    count = 0
    for coin in coins:
        while amount >= coin:
            amount -= coin
            count += 1
    return count


# Example usage:
coins = [1, 5, 10, 25]
amount = 63
```

```
print(coin_change(coins, amount))  # Output: 6 (2
coins of 25, 1 coin of 10, 1 coin of 5, 3 coins
of 1)
```

When to Use Greedy Algorithms vs. Dynamic Programming

While **greedy algorithms** are often faster and simpler to implement, they do not always guarantee the optimal solution for all types of problems. In contrast, **dynamic programming** (DP) guarantees the optimal solution by solving problems using a bottom-up approach, considering all possible solutions and combining the results.

Here are the key differences:

- **Greedy Algorithms**:
    o Make a series of **local optimal choices**.
    o Fast and simple, but not guaranteed to find the global optimum in all cases.
    o Often used in problems that exhibit **greedy choice property** and **optimal substructure**.
    o Examples: Activity selection, Huffman coding, Fractional Knapsack problem.
- **Dynamic Programming**:
    o Solve problems by breaking them down into overlapping subproblems and solving them optimally.

99

- o Guarantee the **global optimal solution**, but typically at a higher computational cost.
- o Used when problems exhibit **optimal substructure** but do not have the **greedy choice property**.
- o Examples: Longest common subsequence, Coin change problem (non-greedy version), Matrix chain multiplication.

In some cases, dynamic programming may be required instead of greedy algorithms. For example, the **Coin Change Problem** where we have **non-standard coin denominations** cannot be solved optimally using a greedy approach, and **dynamic programming** is necessary.

Real-World Example: Network Routing, Task Scheduling

1. Network Routing

In network routing, particularly in scenarios where data needs to be sent from one node to another across a network, **greedy algorithms** are often used. For example, **Dijkstra's algorithm** is a greedy algorithm used to find the shortest path between nodes in a graph. It selects the node with the smallest tentative distance and explores its neighbors, updating their distances, and then repeats this process for the next closest node.

2. Task Scheduling

Task scheduling problems often use greedy algorithms. For example, when scheduling tasks with different priorities and deadlines, the **greedy approach** might involve selecting the task that can be completed the quickest or the one with the earliest deadline. This approach can be used for problems like **interval scheduling** or **job sequencing**.

Exercise: Solving Real-World Greedy Problems

Let's work through an example where we solve a real-world problem using a greedy algorithm: **Interval Scheduling**.

Problem: Given a set of activities, each with a start and finish time, select the maximum number of activities that do not overlap.

Solution:

1. Sort the activities by finish time.
2. Select the first activity, then continue selecting the next activity whose start time is after the finish time of the last selected activity.

python

```python
def interval_scheduling(activities):
```

```python
# Sort activities by finish time
activities.sort(key=lambda x: x[1])

selected_activities = []
last_finish_time = -1

for activity in activities:
    start, finish = activity
    if start >= last_finish_time:

selected_activities.append(activity)
        last_finish_time = finish

    return selected_activities

# Example usage:
activities = [(1, 4), (2, 6), (5, 8), (7, 9), (3,
5)]
print(interval_scheduling(activities))          #
Output: [(1, 4), (5, 8), (7, 9)]
```

Summary of Chapter 9

In this chapter, we explored **greedy algorithms**, which make the best local choice at each step in hopes of finding the global optimum. We examined **activity selection** and the **coin change problem**, both of which can be solved efficiently using a greedy approach.

102

We also discussed when to use **greedy algorithms** versus **dynamic programming**, noting that greedy algorithms are faster but may not always produce optimal solutions. Dynamic programming, while more computationally expensive, guarantees optimal solutions for certain problems.

Real-world applications like **network routing** and **task scheduling** often rely on greedy algorithms to solve complex optimization problems efficiently.

Through a hands-on exercise, we implemented a **greedy algorithm** to solve the **interval scheduling problem**, reinforcing how divide-and-conquer and greedy strategies can be applied in practical scenarios.

In the next chapters, we will delve into more advanced algorithmic techniques such as **backtracking** and **dynamic programming** to solve even more complex problems.

CHAPTER 10

DYNAMIC PROGRAMMING

What is Dynamic Programming? Breaking Down Problems with Overlapping Subproblems

Dynamic programming (DP) is a method used for solving complex problems by breaking them down into simpler subproblems. It is an optimization technique used primarily when the problem has overlapping subproblems and optimal substructure.

- **Overlapping Subproblems**: The problem can be broken down into subproblems that are solved repeatedly. In dynamic programming, we solve each subproblem once and store its solution, avoiding redundant work.
- **Optimal Substructure**: The optimal solution of the problem can be constructed efficiently from the optimal solutions of its subproblems.

The main idea behind dynamic programming is to solve a problem by storing the solutions to its subproblems in a table (or array) so that they don't need to be recalculated each time.

Dynamic programming is used to optimize problems that have **overlapping subproblems** (problems that share subproblems) and **optimal substructure** (the problem can be solved by solving its subproblems optimally).

Examples: Fibonacci Sequence, Longest Common Subsequence

1. Fibonacci Sequence

The **Fibonacci sequence** is a classic example of a problem that can be solved efficiently using dynamic programming. The sequence starts with 0 and 1, and each subsequent number is the sum of the previous two numbers. The naive recursive solution to the Fibonacci sequence leads to redundant calculations, making it inefficient.

- **Naive Recursive Approach**: This approach involves repeated calculation of the same Fibonacci numbers.
- **Dynamic Programming Approach**: We use an array to store the computed Fibonacci values so that each number is calculated only once.

Fibonacci Sequence using Dynamic Programming (Memoization):

python

```python
def fibonacci(n, memo={}):
    if n in memo:
        return memo[n]
```

```
    if n <= 1:
        return n
    memo[n] = fibonacci(n-1, memo) + fibonacci(n-
2, memo)
    return memo[n]

# Example usage:
print(fibonacci(10))   # Output: 55
```

Time Complexity: **O(n)**, where **n** is the input number. This is because we only calculate each Fibonacci number once and store the result in the memo dictionary.

---

2. Longest Common Subsequence (LCS)

The **Longest Common Subsequence (LCS)** problem is another common problem solved using dynamic programming. Given two strings, the goal is to find the longest subsequence (not necessarily contiguous) that appears in both strings.

Dynamic Programming Approach:

- Construct a 2D table to store the lengths of the longest common subsequence for each pair of prefixes of the two strings.

- Build the solution by comparing the characters in both strings and filling in the table based on whether the characters match.

Algorithm:

1. If the characters match, the value is 1 + LCS(i-1, j-1).
2. If the characters do not match, the value is the maximum of LCS(i-1, j) and LCS(i, j-1).

python

```python
def lcs(X, Y):
    m = len(X)
    n = len(Y)

    # Create a 2D table to store results of subproblems
    L = [[0] * (n + 1) for _ in range(m + 1)]

    for i in range(m + 1):
        for j in range(n + 1):
            if i == 0 or j == 0:
                L[i][j] = 0
            elif X[i-1] == Y[j-1]:
                L[i][j] = L[i-1][j-1] + 1
            else:
```

```
        L[i][j] = max(L[i-1][j], L[i][j-
1])


    # The length of the LCS will be in the bottom-
right corner of the table
    return L[m][n]

# Example usage:
X = "AGGTAB"
Y = "GXTXAYB"
print(lcs(X, Y))  # Output: 4 (The LCS is "GTAB")
```

Time Complexity: **O(m * n)**, where **m** and **n** are the lengths of the two strings. This is because we fill a 2D table of size **m × n**.

When to Use Dynamic Programming to Optimize Algorithms

Dynamic programming is used to optimize algorithms that have overlapping subproblems and optimal substructure. Here's when to consider using dynamic programming:

1. **Overlapping Subproblems**: If the problem can be broken down into subproblems that are solved repeatedly, then dynamic programming can optimize the solution by storing the results of previously solved subproblems.

2. **Optimal Substructure**: If the optimal solution to the problem can be constructed efficiently from the optimal

solutions of its subproblems, dynamic programming is a good choice.

Some problems, such as **Fibonacci sequence** and **LCS**, are naturally suited to dynamic programming, while others may require additional insight or modifications to the problem to be efficiently solved with DP.

In general, dynamic programming is used to:

- Avoid recomputing the same results multiple times.
- Solve problems that would otherwise require exponential time (e.g., brute-force recursive solutions) by solving subproblems once and reusing the results.

Real-World Application: Resource Allocation, Optimization Problems

Dynamic programming is widely used in real-world applications, especially in **resource allocation** and **optimization problems** where decisions need to be made step-by-step, and each decision can impact future outcomes.

1. Resource Allocation:

In resource allocation problems, such as budgeting or scheduling, dynamic programming is used to find the optimal allocation of resources over time. For example, the **Knapsack problem** is a classic optimization problem that can be solved using dynamic programming.

2. Optimization Problems:

Dynamic programming is used in optimization problems where you need to find the best solution under certain constraints. For example:

- **Shortest Path**: Finding the shortest path between two nodes in a graph (e.g., using the **Floyd-Warshall algorithm**).
- **Job Scheduling**: Determining the optimal schedule for jobs with different start times, durations, and deadlines.

Dynamic programming is used in fields like **finance** (for portfolio optimization), **operations research**, and **bioinformatics** (e.g., sequence alignment problems).

Exercise: Solving Classic Dynamic Programming Problems

Let's solve a few classic dynamic programming problems to strengthen your understanding of this technique.

1. 0/1 Knapsack Problem

In the **Knapsack problem**, you have a set of items, each with a weight and a value, and a knapsack with a maximum weight capacity. The goal is to determine the maximum value of items that can be placed in the knapsack without exceeding the weight limit.

python

```python
def knapsack(weights, values, capacity):
    n = len(weights)
    dp = [[0] * (capacity + 1) for _ in range(n + 1)]

    for i in range(n + 1):
        for w in range(capacity + 1):
            if i == 0 or w == 0:
                dp[i][w] = 0
            elif weights[i-1] <= w:
                dp[i][w] = max(values[i-1] + dp[i-1][w - weights[i-1]], dp[i-1][w])
            else:
                dp[i][w] = dp[i-1][w]

    return dp[n][capacity]

# Example usage:
weights = [2, 3, 4, 5]
```

```
values = [3, 4, 5, 6]
capacity = 5
print(knapsack(weights,  values,  capacity))    #
Output: 7
```

Time Complexity: **O(n * capacity)**, where **n** is the number of items and **capacity** is the maximum weight of the knapsack. This is because we fill a 2D table of size **n × capacity**.

---

2. Rod Cutting Problem

In the **Rod Cutting Problem**, you are given a rod of length **n** and a list of prices for each length from 1 to **n**. The goal is to find the maximum revenue you can obtain by cutting the rod into pieces and selling those pieces at their respective prices.

python

```
def rod_cutting(prices, n):
    dp = [0] * (n + 1)

    for i in range(1, n + 1):
        for j in range(1, i + 1):
            dp[i] = max(dp[i], prices[j - 1] +
dp[i - j])

    return dp[n]
```

```
# Example usage:
prices = [2, 5, 7, 8, 10]
n = 5
print(rod_cutting(prices, n))   # Output: 12 (cut
the rod into lengths 2 and 3)
```

Time Complexity: **O(n²)**, because for each rod length **i**, we examine all possible sub-lengths **j**.

Summary of Chapter 10

In this chapter, we introduced **dynamic programming**, a powerful technique for solving problems that have overlapping subproblems and optimal substructure. We looked at classic examples like the **Fibonacci sequence** and **Longest Common Subsequence**, which demonstrate how dynamic programming can optimize recursive solutions by storing intermediate results.

We also explored when to use dynamic programming instead of other techniques like **greedy algorithms** and **divide and conquer**, emphasizing that dynamic programming is ideal for problems that involve optimization or resource allocation.

Through hands-on exercises, we implemented classic dynamic programming problems like the **Knapsack problem** and **Rod**

Cutting problem, helping solidify your understanding of the technique.

In the next chapters, we will explore more advanced algorithms and real-world applications that rely on dynamic programming to solve complex optimization problems.

CHAPTER 11

BACKTRACKING ALGORITHMS

Introduction to Backtracking: Exploring All Possible Solutions by Undoing Choices

Backtracking is a general algorithmic technique used to solve problems by exploring all possible solutions to a problem incrementally and undoing (backtracking) when a solution does not work. The core idea is to build up a solution one step at a time, and if a solution is not valid, undo the previous step and try a different option.

Backtracking is often used for problems where:

- There are many potential solutions (sometimes an exponential number of solutions).
- We need to explore all possibilities to find the correct one.
- We need to **prune** (cut off) parts of the search tree that cannot lead to a solution, improving efficiency.

The key steps in **backtracking** are:

1. **Make a choice**: At each step, make a choice or move towards a potential solution.
2. **Explore**: Recursively try to extend the solution by making further choices.

115

3. **Undo (Backtrack)**: If the current solution doesn't work, undo the last choice and try a different option.

Backtracking is often used in problems that involve searching, like puzzles, constraint satisfaction problems, and combinatorial optimization problems.

Examples: N-Queens Problem, Sudoku Solver

1. N-Queens Problem

The **N-Queens problem** is a classic example of backtracking. The problem is to place **N** queens on an **N×N** chessboard such that no two queens threaten each other. This means no two queens can share the same row, column, or diagonal.

- **Backtracking Approach**:
  - Place a queen in a row and try to place queens in subsequent rows, making sure they don't attack each other.
  - If you find a position where placing a queen leads to a conflict, backtrack to the previous row and try the next position.

Algorithm:

1. Try placing a queen in a valid position in the first row.

116

2. Move to the next row and try placing a queen in a valid position.

3. If placing a queen in the current row leads to no valid positions, backtrack to the previous row and move the queen.

4. Repeat until a solution is found or all positions are exhausted.

```python
def is_safe(board, row, col, N):
    # Check if the queen can be placed at board[row][col]

    # Check the column
    for i in range(row):
        if board[i][col] == 1:
            return False

    # Check the upper left diagonal
    for i, j in zip(range(row-1, -1, -1),
range(col-1, -1, -1)):
        if board[i][j] == 1:
            return False

    # Check the upper right diagonal
    for i, j in zip(range(row-1, -1, -1),
range(col+1, N)):
        if board[i][j] == 1:
```

```
            return False

    return True


def solve_n_queens(board, row, N):
    if row >= N:
        return True

    for col in range(N):
        if is_safe(board, row, col, N):
            board[row][col] = 1   # Place queen
            if solve_n_queens(board, row + 1, N):
                return True   # If placing queen
leads to a solution, return True
            board[row][col] = 0   # Backtrack

    return False   # No valid position found for
this row


def print_solution(board):
    for row in board:
        print(" ".join(['Q' if x else '.' for x
in row]))


# Example usage:
N = 4
board = [[0 for _ in range(N)] for _ in range(N)]
if solve_n_queens(board, 0, N):
    print_solution(board)
```

```
else:
    print("Solution does not exist.")
```

Time Complexity: **O(N!)**, as the algorithm explores all possible placements of queens.

---

2. Sudoku Solver

Sudoku is a puzzle where the goal is to fill a 9×9 grid with digits such that:

- Each row contains the digits 1–9 without repetition.
- Each column contains the digits 1–9 without repetition.
- Each of the nine 3×3 subgrids contains the digits 1–9 without repetition.

The **backtracking** approach for Sudoku involves trying to fill the grid one cell at a time, and if a conflict occurs, backtrack by undoing the most recent move.

Algorithm:

1. Find the first empty cell.
2. Try placing each number (1–9) in the empty cell.
3. If the number is valid (i.e., does not conflict with the current row, column, or subgrid), move to the next empty cell and repeat.

4. If a conflict occurs, backtrack by removing the last placed number and trying the next one.

5. If all cells are filled correctly, the Sudoku puzzle is solved.

python

```python
def is_valid(board, row, col, num):
    # Check if the number can be placed in the
row, column, and subgrid
    for i in range(9):
        if board[row][i] == num or board[i][col]
== num:
            return False

    start_row, start_col = 3 * (row // 3), 3 *
(col // 3)
    for i in range(3):
        for j in range(3):
            if board[start_row + i][start_col +
j] == num:
                return False

    return True

def solve_sudoku(board):
    for row in range(9):
        for col in range(9):
```

```
            if board[row][col] == 0:   # Empty
cell
                for num in range(1, 10):
                    if is_valid(board, row, col,
num):
                        board[row][col] = num  #
Place number
                        if solve_sudoku(board):
# Recursively solve the puzzle
                            return True
                        board[row][col] = 0   #
Backtrack if no solution is found
                return False
    return True


def print_sudoku(board):
    for row in board:
        print(" ".join(str(num) if num != 0 else
'.' for num in row))


# Example usage:
board = [
    [5, 3, 0, 0, 7, 0, 0, 0, 0],
    [6, 0, 0, 1, 9, 5, 0, 0, 0],
    [0, 9, 8, 0, 0, 0, 0, 6, 0],
    [8, 0, 0, 0, 6, 0, 0, 0, 3],
    [4, 0, 0, 8, 0, 3, 0, 0, 1],
    [7, 0, 0, 0, 2, 0, 0, 0, 6],
    [0, 6, 0, 0, 0, 0, 2, 8, 0],
```

```
    [0, 0, 0, 4, 1, 9, 0, 0, 5],
    [0, 0, 0, 0, 8, 0, 0, 7, 9]
]

if solve_sudoku(board):
    print_sudoku(board)
else:
    print("No solution exists.")
```

Time Complexity: $O(9^{(N^2)})$, where **N = 9** in this case. This is a high upper bound, but in practice, backtracking with pruning significantly reduces the search space.

Optimizing Backtracking Solutions Using Pruning

Pruning is a technique used to improve the performance of backtracking algorithms. By **pruning** the search tree, we eliminate paths that are guaranteed to lead to invalid solutions. This helps reduce the number of recursive calls and thus improves the efficiency of the algorithm.

Pruning Examples:

1. **N-Queens**: We prune by checking if a queen can be placed in a given column, row, or diagonal before making a choice.

2. **Sudoku**: We prune by checking if placing a number in a cell violates the rules of Sudoku (row, column, or subgrid constraints) before continuing.

Pruning allows backtracking algorithms to avoid exploring irrelevant or infeasible solutions, making them much faster.

Real-World Applications: Puzzle Solving, Pathfinding in Games

1. Puzzle Solving:

Backtracking is often used to solve puzzles, where you need to explore all potential solutions systematically:

- **Sudoku Solvers**: Solving puzzles where numbers must be placed in a grid with constraints.
- **Crossword Solvers**: Filling in a crossword grid based on a set of clues.
- **Maze Solvers**: Finding a path through a maze by exploring all possible routes.

2. Pathfinding in Games:

Backtracking is also used in games, particularly for exploring possible paths in games where you need to find the best route or solution. For example:

- **Finding paths**: Backtracking can be used to explore paths in games or puzzles (e.g., Pac-Man, maze solvers).
- **Decision making**: In games with multiple levels of decisions, backtracking can be used to explore all potential outcomes.

Exercise: Implementing Backtracking Algorithms

Let's implement a backtracking algorithm for a classic problem: **Generating All Possible Combinations of a Given Length**.

The problem is to generate all possible combinations of length **k** from a set of numbers {1, 2, ..., n}.

python

```python
def generate_combinations(n, k):
    result = []
    def backtrack(start, path):
        if len(path) == k:
            result.append(path[:])   # Make a of
the current path
            return
        for i in range(start, n + 1):
            path.append(i)
            backtrack(i + 1, path)   # Explore
with next element
```

```
                path.pop()      # Undo the choice
(backtrack)

    backtrack(1, [])
    return result

# Example usage:
n, k = 4, 2
print(generate_combinations(n, k))    # Output:
[[1, 2], [1, 3], [1, 4], [2, 3], [2, 4], [3, 4]]
```

Time Complexity: **O(C(n, k))**, where **C(n, k)** is the number of combinations (n choose k). This is the number of different combinations of length **k** that can be selected from **n** items.

Summary of Chapter 11

In this chapter, we explored **backtracking algorithms**, which are used to solve problems by incrementally building a solution and undoing choices when a solution doesn't work. We saw examples such as the **N-Queens problem** and **Sudoku solver**, both of which use backtracking to explore all possible solutions.

We discussed **pruning**, a technique that helps optimize backtracking solutions by eliminating infeasible paths early in the process. Real-world applications of backtracking include **puzzle**

solving and **pathfinding in games**, where we need to explore different possibilities to find the correct solution.

Through a practical exercise, we implemented a backtracking algorithm to generate all combinations of a given length, reinforcing how backtracking can be used to explore all solutions to a problem efficiently.

In the next chapters, we will explore other algorithmic techniques and problems, building on the foundation laid in this chapter.

CHAPTER 12

GRAPH ALGORITHMS

Introduction to Graphs: Vertices, Edges, Directed vs. Undirected Graphs

A **graph** is a collection of **vertices** (also called nodes) and **edges** (also called links) that connect pairs of vertices. Graphs are used to represent a wide variety of problems, from social networks to computer networks, routing, and more.

- **Vertices (Nodes)**: The fundamental units of a graph, representing entities such as people in a social network, cities in a map, or routers in a network.
- **Edges (Links)**: The connections between pairs of vertices. Each edge represents a relationship or interaction between two vertices.

Graphs can be classified into different types based on their structure and properties:

1. **Directed Graph (Digraph)**:
   o In a directed graph, edges have a direction. Each edge is represented as an ordered pair of vertices (u, v), where u is the source vertex and v is the destination vertex.

127

- o Example: A **Twitter** follower relationship where one person follows another but the reverse is not necessarily true.

2. **Undirected Graph**:
   - o In an undirected graph, the edges do not have a direction. An edge between vertices u and v means the relationship is bidirectional (u is connected to v and vice versa).
   - o Example: A **Facebook** friendship, where both users are connected equally.

3. **Weighted vs. Unweighted Graphs**:
   - o In **weighted graphs**, each edge has a weight or cost associated with it. This is often used to represent distances, costs, or times.
   - o In **unweighted graphs**, edges do not carry any additional information.

Common Graph Algorithms: Depth-First Search (DFS), Breadth-First Search (BFS)

Two of the most important and widely used algorithms for graph traversal are **Depth-First Search (DFS)** and **Breadth-First Search (BFS)**.

1. Depth-First Search (DFS)

DFS is an algorithm for traversing or searching a graph. Starting at the root (or an arbitrary vertex), DFS explores as far as possible along each branch before backtracking.

- **How DFS Works**:
    1. Start at a node (usually the root or any arbitrary node).
    2. Visit the current node.
    3. Recursively visit all adjacent nodes that have not been visited yet.
    4. If a node has no unvisited adjacent nodes, backtrack and visit the next unvisited node.
- **Time Complexity**: $O(V + E)$, where V is the number of vertices and E is the number of edges in the graph.
- **Space Complexity**: $O(V)$, as it may require storing all vertices in the recursive call stack.

2. Breadth-First Search (BFS)

BFS is an algorithm for traversing or searching a graph that starts at the root node and explores all neighboring nodes at the present depth before moving on to nodes at the next depth level.

- **How BFS Works**:
    1. Start at a node (usually the root or any arbitrary node).

129

2. Visit the current node.

3. Add all unvisited adjacent nodes to a queue.

4. Dequeue nodes from the front of the queue and repeat until all nodes are visited.

- **Time Complexity**: $O(V + E)$, where **V** is the number of vertices and **E** is the number of edges in the graph.

- **Space Complexity**: $O(V)$, as we store all vertices in the queue.

Applications of Graph Algorithms: Social Networks, Web Crawlers

Graph algorithms like DFS and BFS have wide applications across many domains. Below are a couple of real-world examples of how graph algorithms are used:

1. Social Networks:

In social networks (like Facebook, Twitter), **graphs** are used to represent users (vertices) and their relationships (edges). Algorithms like DFS and BFS can be used for:

- **Finding friends of friends**: BFS can be used to find users who are two steps away from a given user.
- **Friendship recommendations**: Using graph traversal to find mutual connections between users.

2. Web Crawlers:

Web crawlers use **graphs** to map out the structure of websites. Each page on the web can be represented as a vertex, and hyperlinks between pages are the edges. Web crawlers:

- Use **DFS** or **BFS** to traverse the web starting from a set of seed URLs.
- Use BFS to explore the pages level by level, ensuring that all reachable pages are visited.

3. Network Routing:

In computer networks, **routing algorithms** use graphs to determine the optimal path for data transmission. The nodes represent routers, and the edges represent the links between them. DFS and BFS can be used to find paths between routers, though more advanced algorithms like **Dijkstra's** or **Bellman-Ford** are typically used for optimal pathfinding.

Exercise: Implementing DFS and BFS for Graph Traversal

Now let's implement **DFS** and **BFS** in Python to explore graph traversal. We'll represent the graph using an **adjacency list**.

1. Implementing Depth-First Search (DFS)

DFS can be implemented recursively using a stack. Below is the Python implementation of DFS using an adjacency list.

python

```python
# Graph represented as an adjacency list
graph = {
    0: [1, 2],
    1: [0, 3, 4],
    2: [0, 5],
    3: [1],
    4: [1],
    5: [2]
}


def dfs(graph, node, visited=None):
    if visited is None:
        visited = set()   # Initialize an empty set to track visited nodes

    visited.add(node)
    print(node, end=" ")

    for neighbor in graph[node]:
        if neighbor not in visited:
            dfs(graph, neighbor, visited)
```

```
# Example usage:
dfs(graph, 0)  # Output: 0 1 3 4 2 5
```

2. Implementing Breadth-First Search (BFS)

BFS can be implemented using a queue. Below is the Python implementation of BFS using an adjacency list.

python

```python
from collections import deque

def bfs(graph, start):
    visited = set()  # To track visited nodes
    queue = deque([start])  # Initialize a queue
with the start node

    while queue:
        node = queue.popleft()

        if node not in visited:
            visited.add(node)
            print(node, end=" ")

            for neighbor in graph[node]:
                if neighbor not in visited:
                    queue.append(neighbor)

# Example usage:
bfs(graph, 0)  # Output: 0 1 2 3 4 5
```

Summary of Chapter 12

In this chapter, we introduced **graph algorithms**, focusing on **Depth-First Search (DFS)** and **Breadth-First Search (BFS)**. We learned that graphs are a versatile data structure that can represent a wide range of problems, from social networks to routing in computer networks.

- **DFS** explores a graph deeply by visiting nodes and their neighbors recursively.
- **BFS** explores a graph level by level, visiting nodes in order of their distance from the starting node.

We also explored **real-world applications** of graph algorithms, including social networks, web crawlers, and network routing, and saw how these algorithms are applied in practice.

Through the **exercise**, we implemented both **DFS** and **BFS** algorithms, reinforcing the concept of graph traversal and the importance of these algorithms in solving real-world problems.

In the next chapters, we will explore more advanced graph algorithms, such as **Dijkstra's algorithm**, **Bellman-Ford**, and *A Search**, which are used for shortest path finding and optimization in graphs.

CHAPTER 13

SHORTEST PATH ALGORITHMS

The Problem of Finding the Shortest Path in a Graph

Finding the **shortest path** in a graph is a fundamental problem in computer science, particularly useful in areas like **network routing**, **GPS navigation**, and **robot motion planning**. The shortest path between two vertices in a graph is the path that minimizes the sum of the edge weights (distances, costs, or times) between them.

Graphs can have:

- **Weighted edges**, where each edge has a weight that represents cost or distance.
- **Unweighted edges**, where all edges are considered equal, but the problem still revolves around finding the shortest route in terms of the number of edges.

There are various algorithms for solving shortest path problems, each suited to different types of graphs and problem constraints.

Dijkstra's Algorithm, Bellman-Ford Algorithm, A Search*

1. Dijkstra's Algorithm

Dijkstra's algorithm is one of the most famous algorithms used to find the shortest path from a single source vertex to all other vertices in a **weighted graph**. It works for graphs with **non-negative weights** and uses a greedy approach to find the shortest path.

- **Time Complexity**: $O(V^2)$ with an adjacency matrix, but can be improved to $O((V + E) \log V)$ using a priority queue (min-heap).
- **Space Complexity**: $O(V)$ for storing distances and the priority queue.

Steps:

1. Start at the source vertex and assign it a distance of 0. All other vertices are assigned an initial distance of infinity.
2. Use a **priority queue (min-heap)** to select the vertex with the smallest tentative distance.
3. Update the distances of all adjacent vertices. If a shorter path is found, update the vertex's distance.
4. Repeat until all vertices are processed.

2. Bellman-Ford Algorithm

The **Bellman-Ford algorithm** is similar to Dijkstra's but can handle graphs with **negative edge weights**. It can also detect negative weight cycles (where the sum of edge weights in a cycle is negative).

- **Time Complexity**: $O(V * E)$, where **V** is the number of vertices and **E** is the number of edges.
- **Space Complexity**: $O(V)$ for storing distances.

Steps:

1. Initialize the distance to the source vertex as 0 and all other distances as infinity.
2. Relax all edges **V-1** times (where **V** is the number of vertices). In each relaxation, if the current distance is greater than the new distance, update it.
3. Check for negative weight cycles by attempting one more relaxation. If any distance changes, a negative cycle exists.

3. A Search Algorithm*

*A Search** is an informed search algorithm that combines the features of **BFS** and **Dijkstra's algorithm**. It uses a heuristic to guide the search toward the goal, making it more efficient than

Dijkstra's algorithm for many types of problems, particularly in **pathfinding**.

- **Time Complexity**: **O(E)**, where **E** is the number of edges, but it can vary depending on the quality of the heuristic.
- **Space Complexity**: **O(V)** for storing vertices and their costs.

Steps:

1. Maintain two lists: one for nodes that need to be evaluated and another for nodes that have already been evaluated.
2. Use a priority queue to explore nodes based on their total cost, which is a combination of the **actual cost** to reach the node and the **heuristic cost** to get to the goal.
3. Explore nodes based on their total estimated cost, and update their costs if a shorter path is found.

Real-World Application: GPS Navigation Systems, Network Routing

Shortest path algorithms have a wide variety of **real-world applications**:

1. GPS Navigation Systems:

- **GPS navigation systems** use shortest path algorithms to calculate the fastest route from one location to another. For example, **Dijkstra's algorithm** or *A Search** can be used to determine the shortest or fastest driving routes, considering traffic, road types, and other factors.
- *A Search** is particularly useful in **real-time systems** where the system needs to make decisions quickly based on real-time data (e.g., traffic conditions).

2. Network Routing:

- **Network routers** use shortest path algorithms to determine the most efficient path for data packets to travel across the network. In this context, algorithms like **Dijkstra's** and **Bellman-Ford** are used in protocols like **OSPF (Open Shortest Path First)** for routing in IP networks.
- These algorithms help determine the best path based on various criteria such as network load, latency, and bandwidth.

Exercise: Implementing Dijkstra's Algorithm

Now, let's implement **Dijkstra's algorithm** to find the shortest path in a graph. We'll use an adjacency list representation for the graph and implement the algorithm using a priority queue (min-heap) for efficiency.

```python
import heapq

def dijkstra(graph, start):
    # Initialize distances with infinity and the
start node with distance 0
    distances = {node: float('inf') for node in
graph}
    distances[start] = 0

    # Priority queue to store (distance, node)
pairs
    priority_queue = [(0, start)]  # (distance,
node)

    while priority_queue:
        current_distance,    current_node    =
heapq.heappop(priority_queue)

        # Skip if we've already found a shorter
path to the node
```

```
        if          current_distance          >
distances[current_node]:
            continue

        # Explore neighbors
        for       neighbor,       weight       in
graph[current_node]:
            distance = current_distance + weight

            # Only consider this new path if it's
shorter
            if distance < distances[neighbor]:
                distances[neighbor] = distance
                heapq.heappush(priority_queue,
(distance, neighbor))

    return distances

# Example graph (adjacency list representation)
# The graph is represented as a dictionary of
nodes where the values are lists of tuples
(neighbor, weight)
graph = {
    'A': [('B', 1), ('C', 4)],
    'B': [('A', 1), ('C', 2), ('D', 5)],
    'C': [('A', 4), ('B', 2), ('D', 1)],
    'D': [('B', 5), ('C', 1)],
}
```

```
# Example usage:
start_node = 'A'
shortest_paths = dijkstra(graph, start_node)
print(shortest_paths)  # Output: {'A': 0, 'B': 1,
'C': 3, 'D': 4}
```

Explanation:

- The graph is represented as an adjacency list where each node points to its neighbors along with the edge weights.
- We use a **priority queue (min-heap)** to efficiently retrieve the node with the smallest tentative distance at each step.
- The `distances` dictionary stores the shortest known distance from the start node to each other node.

Time Complexity: $O((V + E) \log V)$, where **V** is the number of vertices and **E** is the number of edges in the graph. This is because each edge is processed once, and each insertion or extraction from the priority queue takes **$O(\log V)$** time.

Summary of Chapter 13

In this chapter, we explored **shortest path algorithms**, including **Dijkstra's algorithm, Bellman-Ford algorithm**, and *A search**, which are used to find the shortest path between nodes in a graph.

- **Dijkstra's algorithm** is used for graphs with **non-negative edge weights** and is efficient for finding the shortest path from a single source to all other vertices.
- **Bellman-Ford** is used for graphs with **negative edge weights** and can also detect negative weight cycles.
- *A search** is used in pathfinding applications where we have an **estimated heuristic** for the destination, improving efficiency.

We also discussed **real-world applications** such as **GPS navigation systems** and **network routing**, where these algorithms are applied to optimize routes and data transmission.

Through the **exercise**, we implemented **Dijkstra's algorithm** to solve the shortest path problem in a graph, reinforcing the concepts and showing how these algorithms can be used in practical applications.

In the next chapters, we will dive deeper into **graph optimization** and explore other advanced algorithms for problems like **network flow**, **minimum spanning trees**, and more.

CHAPTER 14

MINIMUM SPANNING TREE ALGORITHMS

The Concept of a Minimum Spanning Tree in Weighted Graphs

In a **weighted graph**, a **spanning tree** is a subgraph that includes all the vertices of the original graph and a subset of the edges, without forming any cycles. The **minimum spanning tree (MST)** is a spanning tree in which the sum of the edge weights is as small as possible.

For example, imagine a scenario where you need to connect several cities with roads, and you want to minimize the total cost (e.g., construction cost). In this case, the minimum spanning tree gives you the least expensive way to connect all cities.

- **Key Characteristics of MST**:
    1. **Includes all vertices**: The tree must connect all vertices.
    2. **No cycles**: It must be acyclic, meaning there is only one path between any two vertices.
    3. **Minimum total edge weight**: The sum of the edge weights in the tree should be as small as possible.

144

The **minimum spanning tree** can be useful in applications such as designing efficient networks, optimizing transportation routes, and solving clustering problems.

Kruskal's Algorithm, Prim's Algorithm

Two of the most popular algorithms for finding the minimum spanning tree are **Kruskal's algorithm** and **Prim's algorithm**. Both algorithms guarantee that the edges chosen will form a minimum spanning tree, but they work in different ways.

1. Kruskal's Algorithm

Kruskal's algorithm is a **greedy algorithm** that works by sorting the edges in ascending order by their weights and then adding the smallest edge to the tree that doesn't form a cycle.

- **Steps**:
    1. Sort all edges in increasing order of weight.
    2. Initialize a forest where each vertex is its own tree.
    3. Pick the smallest edge. If it connects two different trees, add it to the MST and combine the two trees.
    4. Repeat until you have **V-1** edges in the MST (where **V** is the number of vertices).

- **Time Complexity**: **O(E log E)**, where **E** is the number of edges. Sorting the edges takes **O(E log E)** time, and the union-find operations for cycle detection take nearly constant time.

2. Prim's Algorithm

Prim's algorithm is another **greedy algorithm** that starts with a single vertex and grows the minimum spanning tree one edge at a time by selecting the smallest edge that connects a vertex in the tree to a vertex outside the tree.

- **Steps**:
    1. Start with an arbitrary vertex and add it to the MST.
    2. Choose the smallest edge that connects a vertex in the MST to a vertex outside the MST.
    3. Add the selected edge to the MST and repeat until all vertices are in the MST.
- **Time Complexity**: **O(E log V)** using a priority queue (min-heap), where **V** is the number of vertices and **E** is the number of edges.

While Kruskal's algorithm is edge-based, Prim's algorithm is vertex-based and grows the MST by connecting vertices.

Real-World Use Case: Designing Efficient Networks (e.g., Connecting Cities)

One of the most common real-world applications of minimum spanning trees is in designing **efficient networks**, such as:

- **Road networks**: To minimize the cost of connecting cities with roads, you can model the problem as a graph where each city is a vertex and each road option between two cities is an edge with a cost. Finding the minimum spanning tree will give you the cheapest way to connect all cities.

- **Telecommunication networks**: In telecommunications, a company wants to build a network of towers to connect all cities. By treating cities as vertices and communication links as weighted edges, we can use MST algorithms to minimize the cost of building the network.

- **Power grid construction**: Utility companies can use minimum spanning tree algorithms to find the most efficient way to connect power plants to the grid, ensuring that the infrastructure is optimized in terms of cost.

Both **Kruskal's** and **Prim's algorithms** are well-suited for network design problems, as they ensure minimal total edge weights, which corresponds to minimizing costs in these scenarios.

Exercise: Implementing Prim's Algorithm to Find a Minimum Spanning Tree

Let's now implement **Prim's algorithm** in Python to find the minimum spanning tree (MST) of a graph. We'll use an **adjacency list** to represent the graph and a **priority queue (min-heap)** to efficiently select the minimum edge.

python

```python
import heapq

def prim(graph, start):
    # Initialize the MST and a set to track
visited vertices
    mst = []
    visited = set()
    min_heap = [(0, start)]  # (weight, vertex)

    while min_heap:
        weight, vertex = heapq.heappop(min_heap)

        if vertex in visited:
            continue

        visited.add(vertex)
        mst.append((vertex, weight))
```

```python
        for    neighbor,    edge_weight    in
graph[vertex]:
            if neighbor not in visited:
                heapq.heappush(min_heap,
(edge_weight, neighbor))

    return mst

# Example graph represented as an adjacency list
graph = {
    'A': [('B', 1), ('C', 4)],
    'B': [('A', 1), ('C', 2), ('D', 5)],
    'C': [('A', 4), ('B', 2), ('D', 1)],
    'D': [('B', 5), ('C', 1)],
}

# Example usage:
start_vertex = 'A'
mst = prim(graph, start_vertex)

# Output the MST (ignoring the first element as
it doesn't represent an edge)
print("Minimum Spanning Tree:")
for vertex, weight in mst[1:]:    # Skip the
starting vertex, as it's not part of an edge
    print(f"Vertex: {vertex}, Weight: {weight}")
```

Explanation:

- We use a priority queue (min-heap) to always select the edge with the minimum weight.
- The algorithm starts from the **start vertex** and iterates through the graph, adding edges to the MST that connect new vertices while ensuring no cycles are formed.
- The resulting **MST** is represented as a list of edges, each of which consists of a vertex and the weight of the edge connecting it to the MST.

Time Complexity: **O(E log V)**, where **E** is the number of edges and **V** is the number of vertices. The priority queue operations (push and pop) take **O(log V)** time, and each edge is processed once.

Summary of Chapter 14

In this chapter, we explored **Minimum Spanning Tree (MST) algorithms**, focusing on **Kruskal's algorithm** and **Prim's algorithm**. We learned that MSTs are essential for problems involving network design and optimization, such as connecting cities with roads or building telecommunication networks.

- **Kruskal's algorithm**: Works by sorting the edges and adding them to the MST if they don't form a cycle.

- **Prim's algorithm**: Expands the MST by adding the smallest edge that connects a vertex in the MST to a vertex outside the MST.

We also explored real-world use cases, such as designing efficient networks for cities and telecommunications, where finding a minimum spanning tree is crucial for minimizing costs.

Through the **exercise**, we implemented **Prim's algorithm** in Python to find the MST of a graph, reinforcing the concepts and demonstrating the practical use of MST algorithms.

In the next chapters, we will explore more advanced algorithms for solving graph-related problems, such as **network flow** algorithms and **shortest path algorithms**.

CHAPTER 15

NETWORK FLOW ALGORITHMS

The Flow Problem: Finding the Maximum Flow in a Network

The **network flow problem** involves finding the maximum flow of a resource (like goods, data, or electricity) from a source to a sink through a network of nodes and edges, each with a given capacity. The goal is to determine the maximum amount of flow that can be pushed through the network from the source to the sink, subject to the capacity constraints of the edges.

A **flow network** is a directed graph where:

- Each edge has a **capacity**, which represents the maximum amount of flow that can pass through the edge.
- There are two special nodes: the **source node** (where flow originates) and the **sink node** (where flow is consumed).

The **maximum flow problem** can be formalized as:

- **Maximizing the flow** from the source to the sink, subject to the constraint that the flow through each edge cannot exceed its capacity.

This problem has numerous applications in real-world scenarios, such as:

- **Network routing**: Determining the maximum amount of data that can be transmitted through a network.
- **Transportation optimization**: Maximizing the amount of goods transported from one location to another via roads, rails, or pipelines.
- **Supply chain management**: Optimizing the flow of goods through a distribution network.

Ford-Fulkerson Algorithm, Edmonds-Karp Algorithm

Two well-known algorithms for solving the **maximum flow problem** are the **Ford-Fulkerson algorithm** and the **Edmonds-Karp algorithm**. These algorithms use the concept of **augmenting paths**, which are paths from the source to the sink where the flow can be increased.

1. Ford-Fulkerson Algorithm

The **Ford-Fulkerson algorithm** is a **greedy** approach to finding the maximum flow in a flow network. It repeatedly searches for an **augmenting path** from the source to the sink, where there is still available capacity. Once an augmenting path is found, the flow is increased along the path, and the capacities are updated.

- **Steps**:
    1. Initialize the flow to 0 for all edges.

2. While there is an augmenting path from the source to the sink:

- Find an augmenting path with available capacity.
- Increase the flow along the path.
- Update the capacities of the edges along the path.

3. The algorithm stops when no augmenting paths can be found.

- **Time Complexity**: The time complexity of Ford-Fulkerson depends on the method used to find augmenting paths. In the worst case, it can be **O(max_flow * E)**, where **E** is the number of edges. This happens when each augmenting path only increases the flow by 1.

2. Edmonds-Karp Algorithm

The **Edmonds-Karp algorithm** is an implementation of the Ford-Fulkerson algorithm that uses **Breadth-First Search (BFS)** to find augmenting paths. By always choosing the shortest augmenting path, Edmonds-Karp ensures that the algorithm terminates in polynomial time.

- **Steps**:

1. Use **BFS** to find the shortest augmenting path from the source to the sink.

2. Once an augmenting path is found, increase the flow along the path and update the capacities.

3. Repeat the process until no more augmenting paths can be found.

- **Time Complexity**: $O(V * E^2)$, where **V** is the number of vertices and **E** is the number of edges. This is because BFS takes $O(E)$ time to find an augmenting path, and the number of augmenting paths is at most $O(E)$.

Real-World Applications: Network Design, Transportation Optimization

1. Network Design

In **network design**, the maximum flow problem is used to optimize the design of computer networks, communication networks, and electrical grids. For example:

- **Data transmission**: In computer networks, we use maximum flow algorithms to optimize the amount of data that can be transmitted through the network while respecting the capacities of the communication links.

- **Routing in telecommunications**: The maximum flow algorithm can help find the optimal way to route data through a set of interconnected routers with varying bandwidth capacities.

2. Transportation Optimization

In **transportation networks**, the maximum flow problem can be used to optimize the flow of goods or people through various routes, such as:

- **Supply chain management**: Ensuring that the maximum possible amount of goods can be transported from suppliers to consumers.
- **Traffic flow optimization**: In urban traffic management systems, maximum flow algorithms can help determine the best traffic routing strategies, reducing congestion and improving efficiency.

Exercise: Implementing Network Flow Algorithms

Now let's implement the **Edmonds-Karp algorithm** to find the maximum flow in a flow network. We will use an adjacency matrix to represent the graph, and we will implement **BFS** to find augmenting paths.

```python
python

from collections import import deque

# Function to perform BFS and find an augmenting
path
```

```python
def bfs(capacity, source, sink, parent):
    visited = [False] * len(capacity)
    queue = deque([source])
    visited[source] = True

    while queue:
        u = queue.popleft()

        for v in range(len(capacity)):
            if not visited[v] and capacity[u][v]
> 0:  # If there's remaining capacity
                queue.append(v)
                visited[v] = True
                parent[v] = u  # Store the path
                if v == sink:  # If we've reached
the sink, return True
                    return True
    return False


# Edmonds-Karp implementation of Ford-Fulkerson
def edmonds_karp(capacity, source, sink):
    # Initialize the flow network with zero flow
    flow = [[0] * len(capacity) for _ in
range(len(capacity))]
    parent = [-1] * len(capacity)
    max_flow = 0

    # Augment the flow while there is an
augmenting path
```

```
    while bfs(capacity, source, sink, parent):
        # Find the maximum flow through the path
found by BFS
        path_flow = float('Inf')
        s = sink
        while s != source:
            path_flow       =       min(path_flow,
capacity[parent[s]][s])
            s = parent[s]

        # Update residual capacities of the edges
and reverse edges
        v = sink
        while v != source:
            u = parent[v]
            capacity[u][v] -= path_flow
            capacity[v][u] += path_flow
            v = parent[v]

        max_flow += path_flow  # Add the flow to
the total flow

    return max_flow

# Example graph (adjacency matrix representation)
# capacity[u][v] represents the capacity of the
edge from u to v
graph_capacity = [
    [0, 16, 13, 0, 0, 0],  # Source node 0
```

```
    [0,  0,  10, 12, 0,  0],    # Node 1
    [0,  4,  0,  0,  14, 0],    # Node 2
    [0,  0,  9,  0,  0,  20],   # Node 3
    [0,  0,  0,  7,  0,  4],    # Node 4
    [0,  0,  0,  0,  0,  0],    # Sink node 5
]


source = 0   # Start at node 0
sink = 5     # End at node 5

max_flow = edmonds_karp(graph_capacity, source,
sink)
print(f"The maximum flow from source to sink is:
{max_flow}")
```

Explanation:

- We use an adjacency matrix to represent the **capacity** of each edge in the graph.
- **BFS** is used to find an augmenting path. It also updates the parent array to store the path found by BFS.
- After finding the augmenting path, we update the flow along that path and adjust the residual capacities of the edges.
- This process is repeated until no more augmenting paths can be found, at which point the algorithm returns the **maximum flow**.

159

Time Complexity: $O(V * E^2)$, where **V** is the number of vertices and **E** is the number of edges. This is due to the **BFS** running in **O(E)** time and being performed at most **O(E)** times.

Summary of Chapter 15

In this chapter, we delved into **network flow algorithms**, particularly focusing on the **maximum flow problem**. We learned that finding the maximum flow in a network is crucial for real-world applications such as **network design** and **transportation optimization**.

We explored two well-known algorithms:

- **Ford-Fulkerson algorithm**, which is the basis for many network flow algorithms.
- **Edmonds-Karp algorithm**, which is a more efficient implementation of Ford-Fulkerson using **BFS** to find augmenting paths.

Through a **hands-on exercise**, we implemented the **Edmonds-Karp algorithm** to solve the maximum flow problem in a flow network, reinforcing the concepts and demonstrating the practical use of network flow algorithms.

In the next chapters, we will explore more advanced graph algorithms, such as **maximum bipartite matching** and **minimum cost flow**, to address a wider range of real-world optimization problems.

CHAPTER 16

STRING MATCHING AND TEXT PROCESSING

Algorithms for String Matching: Knuth-Morris-Pratt (KMP), Rabin-Karp

String matching is a fundamental problem in computer science, where the goal is to find one string (the **pattern**) within another string (the **text**). Efficient string matching is crucial in many applications, such as **search engines**, **data processing**, and **text editors**.

There are several algorithms for string matching, each with its strengths and trade-offs. The two most commonly used and efficient string matching algorithms are **Knuth-Morris-Pratt (KMP)** and **Rabin-Karp**.

1. Knuth-Morris-Pratt (KMP) Algorithm

The **KMP algorithm** is an efficient string matching algorithm that searches for a pattern in a text by utilizing previously matched characters to avoid redundant comparisons. The key insight behind KMP is to **preprocess** the pattern to create a **partial match table** (also known as the **prefix function**), which allows the algorithm to skip unnecessary comparisons.

162

- **Preprocessing**: KMP preprocesses the pattern to construct the prefix table, which tells us how many characters we can safely skip if a mismatch occurs.
- **Time Complexity**: **O(n + m)**, where **n** is the length of the text and **m** is the length of the pattern.
- **Space Complexity**: **O(m)**, where **m** is the length of the pattern.

Steps:

1. Preprocess the pattern to create the prefix table.
2. Traverse the text while using the table to skip ahead when a mismatch occurs.

Example:

python

```python
def KMP_pattern_search(text, pattern):
    # Preprocess the pattern to create the
longest prefix suffix (LPS) array
    def build_lps(pattern):
        lps = [0] * len(pattern)
        length = 0
        i = 1
        while i < len(pattern):
            if pattern[i] == pattern[length]:
                length += 1
                lps[i] = length
```

```
                i += 1
            else:
                if length != 0:
                    length = lps[length - 1]
                else:
                    lps[i] = 0
                    i += 1
        return lps


    lps = build_lps(pattern)
    i = 0  # Pointer for text
    j = 0  # Pointer for pattern
    matches = []


    while i < len(text):
        if pattern[j] == text[i]:
            i += 1
            j += 1
        if j == len(pattern):
            matches.append(i - j)
            j = lps[j - 1]
        elif i < len(text) and pattern[j] !=
text[i]:
            if j != 0:
                j = lps[j - 1]
            else:
                i += 1
    return matches
```

```
# Example usage:
text = "ABABDABACDABABCABAB"
pattern = "ABABCABAB"
print(KMP_pattern_search(text,    pattern))       #
Output: [10]
```

---

2. Rabin-Karp Algorithm

The **Rabin-Karp algorithm** is another string matching algorithm that uses a **hash function** to efficiently compare a pattern against substrings of the text. It hashes the pattern and each substring of the text of the same length, and then compares the hashes.

- **Efficiency**: The algorithm works well when there are many pattern matches or when we need to perform multiple string matching searches.
- **Time Complexity**: $O(n + m)$ on average, but $O(n * m)$ in the worst case (when hash collisions occur frequently).
- **Space Complexity**: $O(1)$.

Steps:

1. Compute the hash of the pattern and the hash of the first substring of the text.
2. Compare the hash of the pattern with the hash of the current substring.

3. If the hashes match, perform a direct character-by-character comparison.

4. Move to the next substring and repeat the process.

Example:

python

```
def rabin_karp(text, pattern):
    d = 256  # Number of characters in the input
alphabet
    q = 101  # A prime number to compute the hash
    m = len(pattern)
    n = len(text)
    p_hash = 0  # Hash value for the pattern
    t_hash = 0  # Hash value for the text
    h = 1  # The value of d^(m-1)
    matches = []

    # Precompute d^(m-1) % q
    for i in range(m - 1):
        h = (h * d) % q

    # Compute the hash of the pattern and the
first window of the text
    for i in range(m):
        p_hash = (d * p_hash + ord(pattern[i]))
% q
        t_hash = (d * t_hash + ord(text[i])) % q
```

```
    # Slide the pattern over the text one by one
    for i in range(n - m + 1):
        if p_hash == t_hash:
            if text[i:i + m] == pattern:
                matches.append(i)

        if i < n - m:
            t_hash = (d * (t_hash - ord(text[i])
* h) + ord(text[i + m])) % q
                if t_hash < 0:
                    t_hash += q

    return matches

# Example usage:
text = "ABABDABACDABABCABAB"
pattern = "ABABCABAB"
print(rabin_karp(text, pattern))  # Output: [10]
```

Text Processing: Searching and Replacing Substrings

Text processing refers to manipulating text strings in a variety of ways. One common task is to **search for substrings** and **replace them** with another substring. This is often used in tasks like:

- **Search engines**: Searching for keywords or phrases within documents.

- **Data validation**: Checking if a text matches a specific pattern (e.g., email validation).
- **Text editors**: Searching and replacing text within documents.

Example: Searching and Replacing Substrings

Here's a simple example of searching for a substring and replacing it with another:

python

```python
def search_and_replace(text, search, replace):
    return text.replace(search, replace)

# Example usage:
text = "The quick brown fox jumps over the lazy
dog."
search = "fox"
replace = "cat"
print(search_and_replace(text, search, replace))
# Output: The quick brown cat jumps over the lazy
dog.
```

Real-World Applications: Search Engines, Data Validation

1. Search Engines:

In **search engines**, efficient string matching algorithms are used to match the user query against a vast amount of indexed text. **Rabin-Karp** and **KMP** algorithms can be used to find relevant documents based on keyword matches or phrases.

- **Indexing**: Search engines build indexes of documents and use string matching algorithms to quickly retrieve documents that contain the user's search terms.
- **Ranking**: After finding matches, search engines rank the documents based on factors like relevance, content quality, and link structure.

2. Data Validation:

String matching is also heavily used in **data validation** tasks:

- **Email Validation**: Checking whether a given email string matches a valid email pattern using regular expressions or other pattern-matching algorithms.
- **Phone Number Validation**: Ensuring a phone number matches the correct format.

Exercise: Implementing String Matching Algorithms

Let's implement the **Knuth-Morris-Pratt (KMP)** and **Rabin-Karp** string matching algorithms to help solidify your understanding.

1. Implementing Knuth-Morris-Pratt (KMP) Algorithm

python

```python
def KMP_pattern_search(text, pattern):
    def build_lps(pattern):
        lps = [0] * len(pattern)
        length = 0
        i = 1
        while i < len(pattern):
            if pattern[i] == pattern[length]:
                length += 1
                lps[i] = length
                i += 1
            else:
                if length != 0:
                    length = lps[length - 1]
                else:
                    lps[i] = 0
                    i += 1
        return lps

    lps = build_lps(pattern)
    i = 0
```

```
    j = 0
    matches = []

    while i < len(text):
        if pattern[j] == text[i]:
            i += 1
            j += 1

        if j == len(pattern):
            matches.append(i - j)
            j = lps[j - 1]
        elif i < len(text) and pattern[j] !=
text[i]:
            if j != 0:
                j = lps[j - 1]
            else:
                i += 1
    return matches


# Example usage:
text = "ABABDABACDABABCABAB"
pattern = "ABABCABAB"
print(KMP_pattern_search(text,    pattern))        #
Output: [10]
```

2. Implementing Rabin-Karp Algorithm

python

```
def rabin_karp(text, pattern):
```

```
    d = 256  # Number of characters in the input
alphabet
    q = 101  # A prime number to compute the hash
    m = len(pattern)
    n = len(text)
    p_hash = 0  # Hash value for the pattern
    t_hash = 0  # Hash value for the text
    h = 1  # The value of d^(m-1)
    matches = []

    for i in range(m - 1):
        h = (h * d) % q

    for i in range(m):
        p_hash = (d * p_hash + ord(pattern[i]))
% q
        t_hash = (d * t_hash + ord(text[i])) % q

    for i in range(n - m + 1):
        if p_hash == t_hash:
            if text[i:i + m] == pattern:
                matches.append(i)

        if i < n - m:
            t_hash = (d * (t_hash - ord(text[i])
* h) + ord(text[i + m])) % q
            if t_hash < 0:
                t_hash += q
```

```
    return matches

# Example usage:
text = "ABABDABACDABABCABAB"
pattern = "ABABCABAB"
print(rabin_karp(text, pattern))   # Output: [10]
```

Summary of Chapter 16

In this chapter, we explored **string matching algorithms** and **text processing** techniques, focusing on the **Knuth-Morris-Pratt (KMP)** and **Rabin-Karp** algorithms. We discussed:

- **KMP Algorithm**: An efficient string matching algorithm that preprocesses the pattern to avoid redundant comparisons.
- **Rabin-Karp Algorithm**: A probabilistic string matching algorithm that uses hashing to quickly find pattern matches.

We also covered real-world applications, such as **search engines** and **data validation**, where these algorithms are essential for efficient pattern searching and text manipulation.

Through **hands-on exercises**, we implemented both the **KMP** and **Rabin-Karp** algorithms to demonstrate their usage and efficiency in practical scenarios.

In the next chapters, we will explore more advanced text processing techniques, such as **regular expressions** and **suffix trees**, for solving more complex text-related problems.

CHAPTER 17

ADVANCED DATA STRUCTURES

Advanced Data Structures: Trie, Segment Tree, AVL Tree, B-Trees

In this chapter, we will explore some **advanced data structures** that go beyond the standard linear and tree structures. These data structures are designed to solve specific types of problems more efficiently, especially in scenarios where fast access, insertion, deletion, or search operations are required.

We will focus on the following advanced data structures:

- **Trie**
- **Segment Tree**
- **AVL Tree**
- **B-Trees**

Each of these data structures has unique properties and is suited for different applications.

---

1. Trie (Prefix Tree)

A **Trie**, also known as a **prefix tree**, is a special type of tree used to store a set of strings, where each node represents a single character. Tries are particularly useful for **string matching, auto-completion**, and **prefix-based queries**.

- **Time Complexity**:
  - **Insert: O(m)**, where **m** is the length of the string.
  - **Search: O(m)**, where **m** is the length of the string.
  - **Space Complexity: O(n * m)**, where **n** is the number of strings and **m** is the maximum length of a string.

Key operations:

1. **Insert**: Insert a string into the Trie by adding characters as nodes.
2. **Search**: Check if a given string exists in the Trie.
3. **Prefix Search**: Find all strings that start with a given prefix.

Applications:

- **Autocomplete**: Suggesting words based on a prefix.
- **Dictionary**: Implementing a dictionary for spell-checking or word matching.

Example of Trie Implementation:

python

```
class TrieNode:
    def __init__(self):
        self.children = {}
        self.is_end_of_word = False


class Trie:
    def __init__(self):
        self.root = TrieNode()

    def insert(self, word):
        node = self.root
        for char in word:
            if char not in node.children:
                node.children[char] = TrieNode()
            node = node.children[char]
        node.is_end_of_word = True

    def search(self, word):
        node = self.root
        for char in word:
            if char not in node.children:
                return False
            node = node.children[char]
        return node.is_end_of_word

    def starts_with(self, prefix):
        node = self.root
        for char in prefix:
            if char not in node.children:
```

```
                return False
            node = node.children[char]
        return True


# Example usage:
trie = Trie()
trie.insert("apple")
trie.insert("app")
trie.insert("bat")

print(trie.search("apple"))    # Output: True
print(trie.search("app"))      # Output: True
print(trie.search("bat"))      # Output: True
print(trie.search("bats"))     # Output: False
print(trie.starts_with("ba"))  # Output: True
```

2. Segment Tree

A **Segment Tree** is a binary tree used for storing intervals or segments. It allows querying sums or other operations over ranges in **logarithmic time**, which is especially useful when dealing with **range queries** or **range updates** in large datasets.

- **Time Complexity**:
    - **Build: O(n)**
    - **Query: O(log n)**
    - **Update: O(log n)**

178

Key operations:

1. **Query**: Find the sum (or other operations like min/max) in a given range.
2. **Update**: Update a value in the array, and propagate the changes in the tree.

Applications:

- **Range Queries**: Sum, minimum, or maximum over a range of elements in an array.
- **Efficient Updates**: Handling updates to ranges of elements in the array.

Example of Segment Tree:

python

```python
class SegmentTree:
    def __init__(self, arr):
        self.n = len(arr)
        self.tree = [0] * (2 * self.n)
        self.build(arr)

    def build(self, arr):
        # Initialize the leaves (the second half
of the tree)
        for i in range(self.n):
            self.tree[self.n + i] = arr[i]
        # Build the internal nodes
```

```python
    for i in range(self.n - 1, 0, -1):
        self.tree[i] = self.tree[i * 2] +
self.tree[i * 2 + 1]

def update(self, idx, value):
    # Set value at position idx (leaf node)
    idx += self.n
    self.tree[idx] = value
    while idx > 1:
        idx //= 2
        self.tree[idx] = self.tree[2 * idx]
+ self.tree[2 * idx + 1]

def query(self, left, right):
    # Query the sum in the range [left,
right)
    left += self.n
    right += self.n
    res = 0
    while left < right:
        if left % 2 == 1:
            res += self.tree[left]
            left += 1
        if right % 2 == 1:
            right -= 1
            res += self.tree[right]
        left //= 2
        right //= 2
    return res
```

```
# Example usage:
arr = [1, 3, 5, 7, 9, 11]
seg_tree = SegmentTree(arr)
print(seg_tree.query(1, 4))   # Output: 15 (sum of
arr[1:4] -> 3 + 5 + 7)
seg_tree.update(2, 6)
print(seg_tree.query(1, 4))   # Output: 16 (sum of
arr[1:4] -> 3 + 6 + 7)
```

---

3. AVL Tree

An **AVL Tree** is a self-balancing binary search tree (BST), where the difference between the heights of the left and right subtrees of any node (called the **balance factor**) is at most 1. This property ensures that the tree remains balanced, providing logarithmic time complexity for search, insertion, and deletion.

- **Time Complexity**:
  - **Search**: **O(log n)**
  - **Insertion**: **O(log n)**
  - **Deletion**: **O(log n)**

Key operations:

1. **Insert**: Insert a new node while maintaining the balancing property.
2. **Delete**: Delete a node and rebalance the tree.

181

3. **Search**: Find a node in the tree.

Applications:

- **Efficient Search Operations**: Used in applications where fast searching, insertion, and deletion are required, such as in databases and indexing systems.

Example of AVL Tree:

python

```python
class AVLNode:
    def __init__(self, key):
        self.key = key
        self.left = None
        self.right = None
        self.height = 1


class AVLTree:
    def insert(self, root, key):
        if not root:
            return AVLNode(key)

        if key < root.key:
            root.left = self.insert(root.left,
key)
        else:
            root.right = self.insert(root.right,
key)
```

```python
        root.height               =            1           +
max(self.get_height(root.left),
self.get_height(root.right))
        balance = self.get_balance(root)

        # Left Left Case
        if balance > 1 and key < root.left.key:
            return self.right_rotate(root)

        # Right Right Case
        if balance < -1 and key > root.right.key:
            return self.left_rotate(root)

        # Left Right Case
        if balance > 1 and key > root.left.key:
            root.left                             =
self.left_rotate(root.left)
            return self.right_rotate(root)

        # Right Left Case
        if balance < -1 and key < root.right.key:
            root.right                            =
self.right_rotate(root.right)
            return self.left_rotate(root)

        return root

    def left_rotate(self, z):
```

```
        y = z.right
        T2 = y.left
        y.left = z
        z.right = T2
        z.height = max(self.get_height(z.left),
self.get_height(z.right)) + 1
        y.height = max(self.get_height(y.left),
self.get_height(y.right)) + 1
        return y

    def right_rotate(self, z):
        y = z.left
        T3 = y.right
        y.right = z
        z.left = T3
        z.height = max(self.get_height(z.left),
self.get_height(z.right)) + 1
        y.height = max(self.get_height(y.left),
self.get_height(y.right)) + 1
        return y

    def get_height(self, root):
        if not root:
            return 0
        return root.height

    def get_balance(self, root):
        if not root:
            return 0
```

```
        return    self.get_height(root.left)    -
self.get_height(root.right)

# Example usage:
avl_tree = AVLTree()
root = None
root = avl_tree.insert(root, 10)
root = avl_tree.insert(root, 20)
root = avl_tree.insert(root, 30)
root = avl_tree.insert(root, 15)
```

4. B-Trees

A **B-tree** is a self-balancing search tree that is particularly useful for systems that read and write large blocks of data, such as **databases** and **file systems**. It generalizes the binary search tree by allowing nodes to have more than two children. B-Trees are designed to work well on disk storage, where the cost of accessing data is high compared to accessing memory.

- **Time Complexity**:
  - **Search: O(log n)**
  - **Insert: O(log n)**
  - **Delete: O(log n)**

Applications:

- **Databases**: B-Trees are used in databases for indexing, allowing for fast queries and updates.
- **File Systems**: B-Trees are used in file systems to manage directories and files efficiently.

When to Use These Advanced Data Structures

- **Trie**: When you need fast search, insertion, and prefix-based matching, such as in **autocomplete**, **spell-checking**, and **dictionary lookup**.
- **Segment Tree**: When you need to perform efficient **range queries** and **range updates** on an array or list, such as in **sum queries** or **minimum/maximum queries**.
- **AVL Tree**: When you need a **self-balancing binary search tree** with efficient search, insertion, and deletion operations, and you need logarithmic time complexity for all operations.
- **B-Trees**: When dealing with large amounts of data that don't fit in memory, such as in **databases** and **file systems**, where fast access to data stored on disk is needed.

Exercise: Implementing and Using a Trie for String Matching

We have already implemented a **Trie** in this chapter. You can now use the Trie data structure for efficient **string matching** and **prefix search**.

Example exercises include:

- Inserting a list of strings into the Trie and performing **prefix searches**.
- Implementing **autocomplete** by finding all words that match a given prefix.

CHAPTER 18

BIT MANIPULATION

Introduction to Bitwise Operations and Optimization Techniques

Bit manipulation involves directly manipulating bits (0s and 1s) of data types like integers. This is one of the most low-level, efficient ways to perform operations on data, as computers inherently process information in binary form. By using **bitwise operations**, you can perform many tasks more efficiently, especially for problems that require frequent changes or queries on individual bits of data.

The bitwise operations include:

- **AND (&)**
- **OR (|)**
- **XOR (^)**
- **NOT (~)**
- **Left Shift (<<)**
- **Right Shift (>>)**

Bit manipulation is widely used in scenarios where performance is critical, as it allows you to optimize both time and space. It's especially useful when dealing with:

- **Memory optimization**

- **Cryptographic algorithms**
- **Error detection and correction**
- **Graphics processing**

Examples of Bitwise Operations

1. Counting Set Bits (1s)

One common problem is counting how many bits in a number are set to 1. This is also called **population count** or **Hamming weight**. There are various ways to do this using bitwise operations.

Method:

- Use the property that n & (n - 1) clears the least significant set bit of n. By repeatedly applying this operation, you can count the number of 1s in the number.

python

```python
def count_set_bits(n):
    count = 0
    while n:
        n = n & (n - 1)    # Clear the least
significant bit
        count += 1
    return count
```

189

```
# Example usage:
num = 29   # Binary: 11101, 4 set bits
print(count_set_bits(num))   # Output: 4
```

Time Complexity: **O(k)**, where **k** is the number of set bits in the number, and this is efficient for small numbers.

2. Finding Odd/Even Numbers Using Bitwise Operations

One of the simplest and most common operations is determining whether a number is **odd** or **even**. Using the bitwise **AND** operation with 1, we can easily check the least significant bit.

- A number is **even** if its least significant bit (LSB) is 0.
- A number is **odd** if its least significant bit (LSB) is 1.

python

```
def is_odd(n):
    return n & 1 == 1

def is_even(n):
    return n & 1 == 0

# Example usage:
print(is_odd(5))    # Output: True
print(is_even(4))   # Output: True
```

Time Complexity: **O(1)**, since we are performing a constant-time bitwise operation.

3. Bitwise AND, OR, XOR

These bitwise operations manipulate the bits of two integers. Let's briefly go over each:

- **AND (&)**: Performs a bitwise **AND** operation, returning a 1 only if both bits are 1.
- **OR (|)**: Performs a bitwise **OR** operation, returning a 1 if at least one bit is 1.
- **XOR (^)**: Performs a bitwise **exclusive OR** operation, returning a 1 if the bits are different.

python

```
a = 5   # Binary: 0101
b = 3   # Binary: 0011

print(a & b)   # Output: 1 (Binary: 0001)
print(a | b)   # Output: 7 (Binary: 0111)
print(a ^ b)   # Output: 6 (Binary: 0110)
```

These operations are useful for tasks such as toggling bits, masking certain bits, and checking if specific bits are set.

4. NOT (~) Operation

The **NOT (~)** operation inverts all bits of a number. If you apply it to an integer n, it will change all 1s to 0s and all 0s to 1s.

python

```
n = 5   # Binary: 0101
print(~n)    # Output: -6 (Binary: 1010, Two's
complement representation)
```

Note: The result of the **NOT** operation on an integer can differ in representation depending on the system's number of bits, as negative numbers are represented in **two's complement** form.

5. Left Shift (<<) and Right Shift (>>)

- **Left shift (<<)**: Shifts all bits of a number to the left by a specified number of positions, effectively multiplying the number by 2^k.
- **Right shift (>>) **: Shifts all bits of a number to the right by a specified number of positions, effectively dividing the number by 2^k.

python

```
n = 5   # Binary: 0101

# Left shift by 1
```

```
print(n << 1)    # Output: 10 (Binary: 1010,
Equivalent to 5 * 2)


# Right shift by 1
print(n >> 1)    # Output: 2 (Binary: 0010,
Equivalent to 5 // 2)
```

Applications:

- **Left Shift**: Can be used to multiply a number by a power of 2.
- **Right Shift**: Can be used to divide a number by a power of 2.

Real-World Applications of Bit Manipulation

1. Cryptography

Bit manipulation is foundational in **cryptography**. Many cryptographic algorithms involve bitwise operations to create secure encryption methods. For example:

- **XOR** is used in stream ciphers for encryption and decryption.
- **Bitwise shifts** are used in hashing algorithms and digital signatures.

2. Error Detection and Correction

In **error detection and correction**, bitwise operations are used to manipulate the bits of data transmitted across a network or stored in memory. For example:

- **Checksums** and **cyclic redundancy checks (CRC)** use bitwise operations to detect errors in data transmission.
- **Hamming codes** use bitwise XOR to detect and correct single-bit errors in data.

3. Graphics and Image Processing

Bit manipulation plays an important role in graphics, especially for operations that involve pixel manipulation:

- **Image compression** techniques often involve using bitwise operations to efficiently store and retrieve image data.
- **Bitmaps** and **pixel data** are often manipulated using bit shifts and AND/OR operations.

4. Optimization in Algorithms

Bit manipulation can optimize many algorithms by:

- Reducing memory usage by representing data as bits rather than full integers or arrays.

- Optimizing specific tasks like finding subsets or combinations by using bit masks, where each bit represents the inclusion or exclusion of an element.

Exercise: Solving Problems Using Bit Manipulation

Let's solve a common problem using bit manipulation: **Find the single number in an array where every other number appears twice.**

This problem can be solved efficiently using the **XOR** operation. Since **a ^ a = 0** and **a ^ 0 = a**, XORing all the numbers together will cancel out the ones that appear twice, leaving only the number that appears once.

python

```python
def find_single_number(nums):
    result = 0
    for num in nums:
        result ^= num   # XOR all the numbers
    return result

# Example usage:
nums = [4, 1, 2, 1, 2]
print(find_single_number(nums))   # Output: 4
```

Explanation:

- We initialize `result` to 0.
- We XOR every number in the array with `result`.
- All numbers that appear twice cancel out (because `a ^ a = 0`).
- The result will be the number that appears only once.

Time Complexity: **O(n)**, where **n** is the number of elements in the array. Each number is processed once.

Space Complexity: **O(1)**, since we only use a constant amount of extra space.

Summary of Chapter 18

In this chapter, we explored **bit manipulation** and its various applications, including:

- **Bitwise operations** such as **AND, OR, XOR, NOT, shift operations**, and how they can be used for tasks like counting set bits, checking odd/even numbers, and performing optimizations.
- **Real-world applications** of bit manipulation in **cryptography, error correction, graphics**, and **algorithm optimization**.

- We implemented practical solutions to problems like counting set bits and finding the unique number in an array using XOR.

Bit manipulation is a powerful tool for optimizing algorithms and solving problems that require efficient manipulation of individual bits. In the next chapters, we will explore further optimization techniques and other advanced topics in algorithms.

CHAPTER 19

COMPUTATIONAL GEOMETRY ALGORITHMS

Introduction to Geometric Algorithms: Convex Hull, Line Intersections

Computational geometry is a field of computer science and mathematics that deals with the study of geometric objects and their properties, with a focus on solving geometric problems using algorithms. These algorithms are essential in various domains such as **computer graphics**, **robotics**, **CAD systems**, and **geographic information systems (GIS)**.

In this chapter, we will explore some fundamental problems in computational geometry, including the **convex hull problem** and the **line intersection problem**, and discuss their real-world applications.

---

1. Convex Hull

The **convex hull** of a set of points is the smallest convex polygon that can enclose all the points. It can be thought of as the shape formed by stretching a rubber band around the outermost points of a point set. The **convex hull** is used in many applications,

198

including pattern recognition, image processing, and collision detection in computer graphics.

Algorithms for Convex Hull:

Several algorithms can be used to compute the convex hull of a set of points:

- **Graham Scan**: This algorithm sorts the points based on their polar angle with respect to a reference point (usually the point with the lowest y-coordinate), and then constructs the convex hull using a stack.
- **Jarvis March** (Gift Wrapping): This algorithm iteratively selects the next point on the convex hull by finding the point with the smallest polar angle with respect to the current point.
- **QuickHull**: A divide-and-conquer algorithm that is analogous to **QuickSort**.

Time Complexity:

- **Graham Scan**: $O(n \log n)$, where **n** is the number of points.
- **Jarvis March**: $O(n h)$, where **h** is the number of points on the convex hull.
- **QuickHull**: $O(n \log n)$ on average, but $O(n^2)$ in the worst case.

Example: Graham Scan for Convex Hull

Here is an example of **Graham Scan** to compute the convex hull of a set of points:

python

```python
import math


# Function to compute the orientation of the
triplet (p, q, r)
# Returns a positive value if counter-clockwise,
negative if clockwise, and 0 if collinear
def orientation(p, q, r):
    return (q[1] - p[1]) * (r[0] - q[0]) - (q[0]
- p[0]) * (r[1] - q[1])


# Function to compute the convex hull using
Graham's scan algorithm
def convex_hull(points):
    points = sorted(points, key=lambda x: (x[0],
x[1]))  # Sort the points by x, then by y

    # Build the lower hull
    lower = []
    for p in points:
        while    len(lower)    >=    2    and
orientation(lower[-2], lower[-1], p) <= 0:
            lower.pop()
```

```
        lower.append(p)

    # Build the upper hull
    upper = []
    for p in reversed(points):
        while   len(upper)   >=   2   and
orientation(upper[-2], upper[-1], p) <= 0:
            upper.pop()
        upper.append(p)

    # Remove the last point of each hull because
it's repeated at the beginning of the other hull
    return lower[:-1] + upper[:-1]

# Example usage:
points = [(0, 0), (2, 2), (1, 1), (3, 3), (2, 1),
(4, 0), (0, 3)]
hull = convex_hull(points)
print(hull)   # Output: [(0, 0), (2, 1), (4, 0),
(3, 3), (0, 3)]
```

Explanation:

- We first sort the points based on their x-coordinate (and y-coordinate for tie-breaking).
- We then construct the lower and upper hulls, adding points while ensuring that the convexity condition is maintained (using the orientation function).

- The final convex hull is obtained by combining the lower and upper hulls.

---

2. Line Intersections

Another key problem in computational geometry is finding **intersections** between line segments. This problem has many applications, including **computer graphics**, **geographical mapping**, and **collision detection** in gaming or simulation.

Algorithms for Line Segment Intersection:

- **Brute Force**: Check all pairs of line segments to see if they intersect. This is inefficient for large datasets.
- **Sweep Line Algorithm**: A more efficient approach where you imagine a vertical line sweeping across the plane from left to right, and you maintain a status of the active line segments that the sweep line intersects.
- **Bentley-Ottmann Algorithm**: A specific implementation of the sweep line algorithm that finds all intersections in $O((n + k) \log n)$ time, where **n** is the number of line segments and **k** is the number of intersections.

Example: Brute Force Line Segment Intersection

For simplicity, here's an example of a brute force approach to check if two line segments intersect:

python

```python
def on_segment(p, q, r):
    # Check if point q lies on line segment pr
    return min(p[0], r[0]) <= q[0] <= max(p[0],
r[0]) and min(p[1], r[1]) <= q[1] <= max(p[1],
r[1])


def orientation(p, q, r):
    # Return the orientation of the triplet (p,
q, r)
    return (q[1] - p[1]) * (r[0] - q[0]) - (q[0]
- p[0]) * (r[1] - q[1])


def do_intersect(p1, q1, p2, q2):
    # Find the four orientations
    o1 = orientation(p1, q1, p2)
    o2 = orientation(p1, q1, q2)
    o3 = orientation(p2, q2, p1)
    o4 = orientation(p2, q2, q1)

    # General case
    if o1 != o2 and o3 != o4:
        return True
```

```python
    # Special cases: checking if the points are
collinear and on the segment
    if o1 == 0 and on_segment(p1, p2, q1):
        return True
    if o2 == 0 and on_segment(p1, q2, q1):
        return True
    if o3 == 0 and on_segment(p2, p1, q2):
        return True
    if o4 == 0 and on_segment(p2, q1, q2):
        return True

    return False

# Example usage:
p1 = (1, 1)
q1 = (10, 1)
p2 = (1, 2)
q2 = (10, 2)

print(do_intersect(p1, q1, p2, q2))   # Output:
False
```

Explanation:

- We calculate the orientation of each pair of triplets formed by the endpoints of the line segments.
- If the orientations of the two line segments differ, the segments intersect.

- Special cases handle collinear points to check if the points lie on the segment.

Real-World Applications: Computer Graphics, Robotics

1. Computer Graphics:

In **computer graphics**, computational geometry is used for:

- **Rendering**: Determining the visibility of polygons and shapes.
- **Collision detection**: Checking if objects (e.g., in 2D or 3D environments) intersect.
- **Pathfinding**: Calculating the shortest paths for movement, considering obstacles.

2. Robotics:

In **robotics**, geometric algorithms are essential for tasks like:

- **Motion planning**: Computing collision-free paths for robots.
- **Robot navigation**: Using geometric algorithms to navigate through environments represented as graphs or grids.
- **Object recognition**: Detecting objects and their shapes in images or real-time camera feeds.

Understanding the Geometry Behind Problems

Before diving into the coding of geometric problems, it is crucial to understand the underlying geometric principles:

- **Convexity**: A set of points is convex if the line segment joining any two points in the set lies entirely within the set.
- **Geometric transformations**: Understanding how transformations like rotations, translations, and scaling affect shapes is essential in geometry.
- **Intersection theory**: Recognizing the conditions under which two geometric objects (like lines, circles, polygons) intersect.

Exercise: Solving Basic Computational Geometry Problems

Let's implement a simple **convex hull problem** using the **Graham Scan** algorithm, as demonstrated earlier. This problem will help you apply geometric principles and learn how to use algorithms efficiently.

Task:

- Given a set of points in a 2D plane, compute the convex hull using the **Graham Scan** algorithm.

- Visualize the result using **matplotlib**.

python

```python
import matplotlib.pyplot as plt

# Function to plot the points and convex hull
def plot_convex_hull(points, hull):
    plt.scatter(*zip(*points),     color="blue",
label="Points")
    hull.append(hull[0])  # Close the hull
    plt.plot(*zip(*hull),          color="red",
label="Convex Hull")
    plt.legend()
    plt.show()

# Example usage:
points = [(0, 0), (2, 2), (1, 1), (3, 3), (2, 1),
(4, 0), (0, 3)]
hull = convex_hull(points)
plot_convex_hull(points, hull)
```

Summary of Chapter 19

In this chapter, we explored the world of **computational geometry algorithms**, with a focus on problems like the **convex hull** and **line segment intersections**. These algorithms have a wide range of applications in fields like **computer graphics** and **robotics**.

- We implemented the **Graham Scan algorithm** to compute the **convex hull** of a set of points.
- We also implemented a simple line intersection algorithm.
- We discussed the real-world applications of these algorithms in **collision detection**, **robot navigation**, and **object recognition**.

Geometric algorithms are foundational in many computational fields, and mastering these techniques opens up possibilities for solving a variety of real-world problems efficiently. In the next chapters, we will explore other advanced algorithms, such as **graph algorithms** and **optimization techniques**.

CHAPTER 20

RANDOMIZED ALGORITHMS

Understanding Randomized Algorithms and Their Use Cases

Randomized algorithms are algorithms that make use of random numbers to influence their behavior or decision-making process. These algorithms often provide good average-case performance or even guarantee correctness with high probability, but they may not always give the same output for the same input, as they rely on random choices.

There are two main types of randomized algorithms:

- **Las Vegas Algorithms**: These always produce the correct result, but their runtime may vary depending on the random choices made. The key is that their correctness is guaranteed.

- **Monte Carlo Algorithms**: These may provide a correct answer with some probability. If the algorithm produces an incorrect result, it is typically due to random error, and the probability of this error can be reduced by running the algorithm multiple times or by adjusting parameters.

Why Use Randomized Algorithms?

Randomized algorithms are often used because:

- **Simplicity**: Many randomized algorithms are easier to implement compared to deterministic counterparts.
- **Efficiency**: In certain cases, randomized algorithms perform better on average, particularly in large-scale data problems.
- **Probabilistic guarantees**: For some problems, it is difficult to find a perfect deterministic algorithm, but randomized algorithms can provide a good approximation with high probability.

Examples of Randomized Algorithms

1. Randomized QuickSort

QuickSort is a widely used sorting algorithm that, in its basic form, picks a pivot element and partitions the array into two subarrays. The pivot is chosen deterministically (typically the first or last element), which may result in poor performance (i.e., $O(n^2)$) time complexity) for certain kinds of input, like sorted or nearly sorted data.

A **randomized version** of QuickSort improves the algorithm's performance by selecting the pivot randomly. This reduces the likelihood of encountering worst-case performance, making the algorithm run on average in $O(n \log n)$ time.

Time Complexity:

- **Best and Average Case**: O(n log n)
- **Worst Case**: $O(n^2)$ (though this is highly unlikely with random pivot selection)

Randomized QuickSort Example:

python

```python
import random

def randomized_partition(arr, low, high):
    # Randomly choose a pivot and swap with the
last element
    pivot_idx = random.randint(low, high)
    arr[pivot_idx], arr[high] = arr[high],
arr[pivot_idx]
    pivot = arr[high]

    i = low - 1
    for j in range(low, high):
        if arr[j] <= pivot:
            i += 1
            arr[i], arr[j] = arr[j], arr[i]
    arr[i + 1], arr[high] = arr[high], arr[i + 1]
    return i + 1

def randomized_quick_sort(arr, low, high):
    if low < high:
        pivot_index = randomized_partition(arr,
low, high)
```

```
        randomized_quick_sort(arr,              low,
pivot_index - 1)
        randomized_quick_sort(arr, pivot_index +
1, high)

# Example usage:
arr = [10, 7, 8, 9, 1, 5]
randomized_quick_sort(arr, 0, len(arr) - 1)
print(arr)   # Output: [1, 5, 7, 8, 9, 10]
```

2. Monte Carlo Methods

Monte Carlo methods are a class of algorithms that rely on random sampling to obtain numerical results. These methods are typically used to solve problems that may be deterministic in principle but are difficult or impossible to solve directly.

For example, **Monte Carlo simulations** can be used to estimate the value of complex mathematical expressions (like integrals or probabilities), model systems with uncertainty, or solve optimization problems.

In **Monte Carlo integration**, you estimate the value of an integral by randomly sampling points and computing the average value of the function at those points.

Monte Carlo Simulation Example (Estimating π):

The classic example of a Monte Carlo method is estimating the value of π by simulating random points in a unit square and counting how many fall within a unit circle inscribed inside the square.

Approach:

1. Generate random points within a square of side length 1.
2. Count how many points fall inside the unit circle (where the distance from the origin to the point is less than 1).
3. The ratio of points inside the circle to total points approximates $\pi/4$, so multiplying this ratio by 4 gives an estimate of π.

python

```python
import random
import math

def monte_carlo_pi(num_samples):
    inside_circle = 0
    for _ in range(num_samples):
        x, y = random.uniform(0, 1), random.uniform(0, 1)
        if x*x + y*y <= 1:  # Check if the point is inside the unit circle
            inside_circle += 1
```

```
    return (inside_circle / num_samples) * 4

# Example usage:
num_samples = 1000000
pi_estimate = monte_carlo_pi(num_samples)
print(f"Estimated value of π: {pi_estimate}")
```

Explanation:

- We generate random points in the unit square by choosing random x and y coordinates between 0 and 1.
- We check if the point lies inside the unit circle using the equation $x2+y2\leq1$ $x^2 + y^2 \leq 1$ $x2+y2\leq1$.
- The ratio of points inside the circle to the total number of points gives an estimate of π.

Real-World Applications: Random Sampling, Cryptography

1. Random Sampling

Random sampling is a technique used to select a subset of items from a larger dataset, where each item has an equal chance of being selected. This technique is widely used in:

- **Statistical analysis**: To estimate parameters of a population based on a random sample.

- **Machine learning**: Random sampling is used in algorithms like **random forests** and **bootstrap aggregation (bagging)**.
- **Data compression**: In algorithms like **Bloom filters**, where a probabilistic test is used for membership in a set.

2. Cryptography

In **cryptography**, many algorithms rely on randomness to ensure security. For example:

- **Key generation**: Cryptographic systems often rely on random numbers to generate encryption keys, such as in the case of **RSA** or **AES**.
- **Randomized algorithms** are also used in protocols like **zero-knowledge proofs**, where randomness is used to validate a claim without revealing the underlying information.

Exercise: Implementing a Randomized Algorithm

Let's implement a simple randomized algorithm: **Randomized Selection**, which is a variation of the **QuickSelect** algorithm. The goal of this algorithm is to find the **k-th smallest element** in an unordered list.

Randomized Selection (QuickSelect):

- Similar to QuickSort, but instead of sorting the entire array, you only recurse into the part of the array that contains the k-th smallest element.

python

```python
import random

def randomized_partition(arr, low, high):
    pivot_idx = random.randint(low, high)
    arr[pivot_idx], arr[high] = arr[high], arr[pivot_idx]
    pivot = arr[high]
    i = low - 1
    for j in range(low, high):
        if arr[j] <= pivot:
            i += 1
            arr[i], arr[j] = arr[j], arr[i]
    arr[i + 1], arr[high] = arr[high], arr[i + 1]
    return i + 1

def randomized_select(arr, low, high, k):
    if low == high:
        return arr[low]

    pivot_idx = randomized_partition(arr, low, high)
```

```
    if k == pivot_idx:
        return arr[k]
    elif k < pivot_idx:
        return    randomized_select(arr,    low,
pivot_idx - 1, k)
    else:
        return randomized_select(arr, pivot_idx
+ 1, high, k)


# Example usage:
arr = [12, 3, 5, 7, 19, 4, 1]
k = 3  # Find the 3rd smallest element (index 2)
print(randomized_select(arr, 0, len(arr) - 1, k
- 1))  # Output: 5
```

Explanation:

- We first choose a pivot element randomly using the **randomized_partition** function, which partitions the array.
- Then, based on the position of the pivot, we decide whether to continue searching to the left or right of the pivot to find the **k-th smallest element**.

Time Complexity: On average, the **O(n)** complexity holds, but in the worst case, it can degrade to **O(n²)**, similar to QuickSort.

Summary of Chapter 20

In this chapter, we explored **randomized algorithms**, focusing on their practical use and how randomness can be leveraged to simplify problem-solving. We discussed:

- **Randomized QuickSort**: A version of QuickSort that uses random pivots to improve performance.
- **Monte Carlo methods**: A class of algorithms that rely on random sampling to solve problems such as estimating π.
- **Applications** in fields like **cryptography**, **random sampling**, and **optimization**.

Through a hands-on exercise, we implemented **Randomized Selection (QuickSelect)**, demonstrating how randomness can be used to find the k-th smallest element in an array efficiently.

Randomized algorithms provide a powerful toolset for solving problems, especially when deterministic solutions are too slow or complex. In the next chapters, we will explore more advanced topics and further techniques for optimization and approximation.

CHAPTER 21

OPTIMIZATION ALGORITHMS

Introduction to Optimization: Finding the Best Solution to a Problem

Optimization is the process of finding the best solution to a problem from a set of possible solutions, often subject to certain constraints. In computational terms, an optimization problem involves minimizing or maximizing a function, which represents a cost or objective. This function is called the **objective function**, and the solution space consists of all the possible values that the variables can take.

Optimization problems are widespread across various fields, including economics, engineering, logistics, and artificial intelligence. There are different types of optimization problems, such as:

- **Linear Optimization**: Problems where the objective function and constraints are linear.
- **Nonlinear Optimization**: Problems where the objective function or constraints are nonlinear.
- **Combinatorial Optimization**: Problems involving discrete decisions, such as finding the shortest path or selecting the best subset of items.

Optimization algorithms are designed to solve these problems efficiently. In this chapter, we will discuss some well-known optimization techniques and their applications.

Examples of Optimization Algorithms

1. Linear Programming (LP)

Linear programming is an optimization technique used to solve problems where the objective function and constraints are linear. The general form of a linear programming problem is:

- Maximize (or Minimize): $c1x1+c2x2+\cdots+cnxnc\_1x\_1 + c\_2x\_2 + \dots + c\_nx\_nc1x1+c2x2+\cdots+cnxn$

- Subject to constraints:

  $a11x1+a12x2+\cdots+a1nxn{\leq}b1a\_{11}x\_1 + a\_{12}x\_2 + \dots + a\_{1n}x\_n \leq b\_1a11x1+a12x2+\cdots+a1nxn{\leq}b1$
  $a21x1+a22x2+\cdots+a2nxn{\leq}b2a\_{21}x\_1 + a\_{22}x\_2 + \dots + a\_{2n}x\_n \leq b\_2a21x1+a22x2+\cdots+a2nxn{\leq}b2$
  $\vdots$ $x1,x2,\dots,xn{\geq}0x\_1, x\_2, \dots, x\_n \geq 0x1,x2,\dots,xn{\geq}0$

Linear programming is widely used in fields such as economics, business planning, transportation, and manufacturing.

Algorithms:

- **Simplex Method**: A popular method for solving LP problems that iterates over the vertices of the feasible region.
- **Interior Point Methods**: These methods solve the LP problem by moving through the interior of the feasible region.

Example of Linear Programming:

Using the **PuLP** library in Python, we can solve a simple linear programming problem.

python

```
from pulp import LpMaximize, LpProblem, LpVariable

# Define the problem
problem = LpProblem("Maximize_Cost", LpMaximize)

# Define the decision variables
x = LpVariable("x", lowBound=0)
y = LpVariable("y", lowBound=0)

# Define the objective function
problem += 3 * x + 2 * y   # Maximize 3x + 2y

# Define the constraints
problem += x + y <= 4
```

```
problem += x - 2 * y >= 1

# Solve the problem
problem.solve()

# Get the results
print(f"Optimal value of x: {x.varValue}")
print(f"Optimal value of y: {y.varValue}")
```

In this example, we are solving a linear optimization problem where we maximize the objective function 3x+2y3x + 2y3x+2y, subject to two constraints. The `PuLP` library is a powerful tool for solving LP problems in Python.

---

2. Simulated Annealing

Simulated Annealing (SA) is a probabilistic optimization algorithm inspired by the physical process of heating and then slowly cooling a material to increase the size of its crystals and reduce defects. In optimization, the algorithm explores the solution space by accepting new solutions with a probability that decreases over time. This helps avoid getting stuck in local optima.

The key idea is to:

1. Start with an initial solution.

2. Make small random changes (moves) to the solution.

3. Accept the new solution if it improves the objective, or accept it with a certain probability if it worsens.

4. Gradually decrease the probability of accepting worse solutions (analogous to lowering the temperature in annealing).

Simulated annealing is particularly useful for **nonlinear optimization** problems with a large search space.

Time Complexity: In general, **O(n)** for each iteration, where **n** is the size of the solution space. The total number of iterations depends on the cooling schedule.

Example of Simulated Annealing:
python

```python
import random
import math

# Objective function (example: minimize f(x) = (x
- 3)^2)
def objective_function(x):
    return (x - 3)**2


# Simulated Annealing function
def simulated_annealing(start, end, max_iter,
temp_start, temp_end):
    current_solution = start
```

```
    current_value                          =
objective_function(current_solution)
    best_solution = current_solution
    best_value = current_value
    temperature = temp_start

    for _ in range(max_iter):
        # Generate a random neighbor
        neighbor      =      current_solution      +
random.uniform(-1, 1)
        neighbor_value                         =
objective_function(neighbor)

        # Calculate acceptance probability
        if neighbor_value < current_value:
            current_solution = neighbor
            current_value = neighbor_value
        else:
            acceptance_probability             =
math.exp((current_value  -  neighbor_value)  /
temperature)
            if        random.random()           <
acceptance_probability:
                current_solution = neighbor
                current_value = neighbor_value

        # Update the best solution found so far
        if current_value < best_value:
            best_solution = current_solution
```

```
        best_value = current_value

    # Cool down
    temperature = temperature * (temp_end /
temp_start) ** (1 / max_iter)

    return best_solution, best_value

# Example usage:
best_solution,           best_value           =
simulated_annealing(start=0,              end=5,
max_iter=1000, temp_start=100, temp_end=0.01)
print(f"Best   solution:   {best_solution},   Best
value: {best_value}")
```

In this example, we use simulated annealing to find the minimum of the function $f(x)=(x-3)2f(x) = (x - 3)^2f(x)=(x-3)2$. The algorithm starts at a random value and gradually moves toward the global minimum by probabilistically accepting new solutions.

---

3. Genetic Algorithms

Genetic Algorithms (GA) are search heuristics that simulate the process of natural evolution. They are used to find approximate solutions to optimization and search problems. The algorithm iterates through a population of possible solutions, selecting individuals (solutions) based on their fitness, and combining them (using crossover) to form new individuals. Mutations are applied to add diversity.

Basic Steps:

1. **Initialization**: Create a random population of individuals.
2. **Selection**: Evaluate the fitness of each individual and select parents for reproduction.
3. **Crossover**: Combine parents to produce offspring.
4. **Mutation**: Apply small random changes to the offspring.
5. **Replacement**: Replace the old population with the new one.
6. Repeat the process for a specified number of generations.

Example of Genetic Algorithm:

python

```python
import random


# Define the objective function (e.g., maximize
f(x) = x^2)
def objective_function(x):
    return x**2


# Crossover function: one-point crossover
def crossover(parent1, parent2):
    crossover_point   =    random.randint(1,
len(parent1) - 1)
```

```python
    offspring1 = parent1[:crossover_point] +
parent2[crossover_point:]
    offspring2 = parent2[:crossover_point] +
parent1[crossover_point:]
    return offspring1, offspring2


# Mutation function: randomly change one bit of
the individual
def mutate(individual):
    mutation_point = random.randint(0,
len(individual) - 1)
    individual[mutation_point] = 1 -
individual[mutation_point]  # Flip the bit
    return individual


# Selection function: Select the best individuals
based on their fitness
def selection(population, fitness_values):
    selected = random.choices(population,
weights=fitness_values, k=len(population)//2)
    return selected


# Genetic Algorithm
def genetic_algorithm(population_size,
generations, mutation_rate):
    population = [[random.randint(0, 1) for _ in
range(8)] for _ in range(population_size)]
    best_solution = None
    best_fitness = -float('inf')
```

227

```python
for generation in range(generations):
    fitness_values                            =
[objective_function(int("".join(map(str,   ind)),
2)) for ind in population]
    new_population = []

    # Selection
    selected_parents = selection(population,
fitness_values)

    # Crossover and mutation
    for i in range(0, len(selected_parents),
2):
        parent1,          parent2          =
selected_parents[i], selected_parents[i + 1]
        offspring1,        offspring2       =
crossover(parent1, parent2)

        if random.random() < mutation_rate:
            offspring1 = mutate(offspring1)
        if random.random() < mutation_rate:
            offspring2 = mutate(offspring2)

        new_population.extend([offspring1,
offspring2])

    population = new_population
```

```
        # Track the best solution
        best_genetic_value = max(fitness_values)
        if best_genetic_value > best_fitness:
            best_fitness = best_genetic_value
            best_solution                        =
population[fitness_values.index(best_genetic_va
lue)]


    return best_solution, best_fitness


# Example usage:
best_solution,              best_fitness        =
genetic_algorithm(population_size=100,
generations=50, mutation_rate=0.01)
print(f"Best    solution:    {best_solution},    Best
fitness: {best_fitness}")
```

In this example, we use a genetic algorithm to maximize $f(x)=x2 f(x) = x^2 f(x)=x2$ by evolving a population of binary strings. Each individual in the population represents a number, and the algorithm tries to find the highest number by evolving the population through selection, crossover, and mutation.

Real-World Applications: Machine Learning, Operational Research

1. Machine Learning

In **machine learning**, optimization algorithms are used to:

- **Train models**: Optimizing the parameters of a machine learning model (e.g., weights in neural networks) using gradient descent or genetic algorithms.
- **Hyperparameter tuning**: Finding the best set of hyperparameters for a model, such as the learning rate, regularization parameters, etc.

2. Operational Research

In **operational research**, optimization techniques are used to:

- **Supply chain management**: Optimizing logistics and inventory management.
- **Scheduling**: Allocating resources (e.g., employees, machines) to tasks to minimize costs or time.
- **Transportation problems**: Finding the optimal route or distribution of goods to minimize costs.

Exercise: Solving Optimization Problems with Python

In this exercise, we solved optimization problems using three different algorithms: **Linear Programming**, **Simulated Annealing**, and **Genetic Algorithms**. The problems demonstrated how to apply these optimization techniques to find the best solutions for real-world problems, such as maximizing an objective function or minimizing costs.

Through these examples, we saw how **optimization** plays a crucial role in improving efficiency and decision-making in various fields. You can implement these algorithms in Python to solve more complex optimization problems based on your specific use case.

In the next chapters, we will explore more advanced optimization techniques and real-world applications in AI and data science.

CHAPTER 22

APPROXIMATION ALGORITHMS

When Exact Solutions Aren't Feasible, Using Approximation Algorithms

In many real-world problems, finding an **exact solution** may be computationally expensive or infeasible due to the size or complexity of the problem. For example, in large-scale problems such as routing, scheduling, or resource allocation, **exact solutions** can take an impractically long time to compute. In such cases, **approximation algorithms** are used to find near-optimal solutions in a much shorter time.

Approximation algorithms are algorithms that provide solutions that are guaranteed to be close to the optimal solution. These algorithms are particularly useful for **NP-hard** problems, where finding an exact solution is computationally expensive.

The key features of approximation algorithms are:

- **Efficiency**: They provide a solution in polynomial time, unlike exact algorithms that may take exponential time for large instances.

- **Proximity to Optimal Solution**: They guarantee that the solution is within a specific factor of the optimal solution, called the **approximation ratio**.

Examples of Approximation Algorithms

1. Traveling Salesman Problem (TSP)

The **Traveling Salesman Problem (TSP)** is one of the most famous **NP-hard** problems. The objective is to find the shortest possible route that visits each city exactly once and returns to the origin city.

- **Exact Solution**: The exact solution requires evaluating all possible permutations of cities, which takes factorial time, making it impractical for large numbers of cities.
- **Approximation Algorithm**: One of the simplest approximation algorithms for TSP is the **Nearest Neighbor Algorithm**, where you start at a random city and always travel to the nearest unvisited city. This algorithm provides a **2-approximation** for TSP, meaning the solution will be at most twice the length of the optimal solution.

Nearest Neighbor Algorithm for TSP:

python

```python
import random
```

```python
def nearest_neighbor(cities):
    n = len(cities)
    visited = [False] * n
    tour = [0]  # Start at city 0
    visited[0] = True
    total_distance = 0

    for _ in range(n - 1):
        last_visited = tour[-1]
        nearest_city = None
        nearest_distance = float('inf')

        for i in range(n):
            if not visited[i]:
                dist                       =
abs(cities[last_visited][0]  -  cities[i][0])  +
abs(cities[last_visited][1] - cities[i][1])
                if dist < nearest_distance:
                    nearest_distance = dist
                    nearest_city = i

        tour.append(nearest_city)
        visited[nearest_city] = True
        total_distance += nearest_distance

    # Return to the starting city
    total_distance += abs(cities[tour[-1]][0] -
cities[tour[0]][0]) + abs(cities[tour[-1]][1] -
cities[tour[0]][1])
```

```
    return tour, total_distance

# Example usage:
cities = [(0, 0), (1, 2), (2, 4), (3, 1), (4, 3)]
tour, total_distance = nearest_neighbor(cities)
print(f"Tour: {tour}")
print(f"Total Distance: {total_distance}")
```

In this example:

- The algorithm starts at a random city and selects the nearest unvisited city at each step.
- We calculate the total distance by summing the distances between consecutive cities in the tour.

Time Complexity: $O(n^2)$, where **n** is the number of cities. For each city, we check all other cities to find the nearest neighbor.

---

2. Vertex Cover Problem

The **Vertex Cover Problem** is another NP-hard problem. In a graph, a vertex cover is a set of vertices such that every edge in the graph has at least one endpoint in the set. The objective is to find the smallest possible vertex cover.

- **Exact Solution**: The exact solution requires checking all subsets of vertices, which is computationally infeasible for large graphs.

- **Approximation Algorithm**: A simple **greedy algorithm** can be used to approximate the solution. The algorithm selects an edge, adds both its endpoints to the vertex cover, and removes all edges incident to these vertices. This continues until all edges are covered.

Greedy Vertex Cover Algorithm:

python

```python
def greedy_vertex_cover(graph):
    vertex_cover = set()
    edges = list(graph.keys())

    while edges:
        edge = edges.pop()
        u, v = edge

        if u not in vertex_cover and v not in vertex_cover:
            vertex_cover.add(u)
            vertex_cover.add(v)

        # Remove all edges covered by u or v
        edges = [e for e in edges if u not in e and v not in e]

    return vertex_cover
```

```
# Example usage:
graph = {
    (0, 1): {},
    (0, 2): {},
    (1, 3): {},
    (2, 3): {}
}
vertex_cover = greedy_vertex_cover(graph)
print(f"Vertex Cover: {vertex_cover}")
```

In this example:

- The algorithm selects an edge, adds both endpoints to the vertex cover, and removes edges covered by these vertices.
- It repeats this until all edges are covered.

Time Complexity: **O(E)**, where **E** is the number of edges. Each edge is processed once, and we check each vertex only when it is added to the vertex cover.

Real-World Applications: Scheduling, Routing, Resource Allocation

1. Scheduling

Approximation algorithms are frequently used in **scheduling problems**, where we need to assign tasks to resources (e.g., machines, workers) in an optimal or near-optimal way. Examples include:

- **Job Scheduling**: Minimizing the total completion time of tasks.
- **Multiprocessor Scheduling**: Assigning tasks to multiple processors with constraints on time or resources.

2. Routing

In **routing problems**, such as the **Traveling Salesman Problem (TSP)** or **vehicle routing problems**, approximation algorithms are used to find near-optimal solutions. This is especially important in logistics and delivery systems where the goal is to minimize travel time or cost.

3. Resource Allocation

Approximation algorithms are useful in **resource allocation problems**, such as:

- **Load balancing**: Distributing workloads across multiple servers to optimize resource utilization.
- **Network design**: Optimizing the placement of resources in communication networks to minimize cost or maximize efficiency.

Exercise: Implementing an Approximation Algorithm

Let's implement a simple approximation algorithm for the **Set Cover Problem**, which is another NP-hard problem. The objective is to select a minimum number of sets from a collection of sets such that their union covers all elements in a universal set. A greedy approximation algorithm can be used to select sets based on their contribution to covering uncovered elements.

Greedy Set Cover Algorithm:

python

```python
def greedy_set_cover(universe, sets):
    cover = set()
    selected_sets = []

    while cover != universe:
        # Select the set that covers the most
uncovered elements
        best_set = None
        best_cover = 0

        for s in sets:
            uncovered_elements = s - cover
            if    len(uncovered_elements)     >
best_cover:
                best_set = s
```

```
                    best_cover               =
len(uncovered_elements)

        cover |= best_set
        selected_sets.append(best_set)
        sets.remove(best_set)

    return selected_sets

# Example usage:
universe = {1, 2, 3, 4, 5, 6}
sets = [{1, 2, 3}, {1, 4}, {2, 5}, {3, 6}, {4, 5,
6}]
selected_sets = greedy_set_cover(universe, sets)
print(f"Selected sets: {selected_sets}")
```

In this example:

- We are given a universe of elements and a collection of sets.
- The greedy algorithm selects the set that covers the most uncovered elements in each iteration, until all elements are covered.

Time Complexity: **O(m * n)**, where **m** is the number of sets and **n** is the number of elements in the universe. For each set, we check how many uncovered elements it covers.

240

Summary of Chapter 22

In this chapter, we explored **approximation algorithms**, which provide near-optimal solutions to problems where finding an exact solution is computationally expensive or infeasible. We discussed:

- **Traveling Salesman Problem (TSP)** and its **nearest neighbor algorithm** approximation.
- **Vertex Cover Problem** and the **greedy approximation** algorithm for finding a vertex cover.
- Real-world applications in **scheduling**, **routing**, and **resource allocation**.

Through hands-on exercises, we implemented several approximation algorithms, including **greedy set cover** and **nearest neighbor TSP**, to demonstrate how these techniques can be applied to solve complex problems efficiently.

Approximation algorithms play a crucial role in many fields, from logistics to machine learning, and are essential tools for tackling large-scale optimization problems where exact solutions are impractical. In the next chapters, we will explore more advanced algorithms and techniques for solving optimization problems.

CHAPTER 23

PARALLEL ALGORITHMS

Introduction to Parallel Computing and Algorithms

Parallel computing refers to the simultaneous execution of multiple computations or tasks to solve a problem faster or more efficiently. This approach leverages multiple processors or cores to perform different parts of a computation simultaneously, thereby reducing the overall time needed to complete a task.

Parallel algorithms are designed to take advantage of parallel computing architectures (e.g., multi-core processors, clusters, or GPUs) by dividing a problem into smaller, independent tasks that can be processed concurrently. These algorithms are crucial in solving large-scale problems that are computationally expensive and would otherwise take too long to solve on a single processor.

Key concepts in parallel computing and parallel algorithms include:

- **Concurrency**: The ability to perform multiple tasks simultaneously but not necessarily in parallel.
- **Parallelism**: The simultaneous execution of multiple tasks in parallel, typically on multiple cores or processors.

- **Speedup**: The measure of how much faster a parallel algorithm is compared to its sequential counterpart.
- **Scalability**: The ability of an algorithm to efficiently utilize an increasing number of processors.

Concepts of Divide-and-Conquer in Parallel Environments

One of the most common paradigms used in parallel algorithms is **divide-and-conquer**. This technique divides a problem into smaller subproblems, solves them independently (often in parallel), and then combines the solutions of the subproblems to solve the original problem. Parallel computing significantly enhances the efficiency of divide-and-conquer algorithms by executing the subproblems concurrently.

Divide-and-Conquer in Parallel:

1. **Divide**: Split the problem into smaller subproblems.
2. **Conquer**: Solve each subproblem in parallel (independently).
3. **Combine**: Merge the solutions of the subproblems to form the final solution.

Common problems where divide-and-conquer parallel algorithms are used include:

- **Sorting** (e.g., **parallel merge sort**)

- **Matrix multiplication**
- **Searching** (e.g., **parallel binary search**)
- **Image processing** (e.g., **parallel filtering**)

Parallel divide-and-conquer algorithms are effective when subproblems are independent and can be solved simultaneously.

Real-World Applications: Image Processing, Data Analysis

1. Image Processing

In **image processing**, many tasks, such as filtering, transforming, or resizing images, can be parallelized to improve performance. For example:

- **Image filtering**: Involves applying a filter (such as a blur or sharpening filter) to every pixel in an image. This task is easily parallelizable, as each pixel's new value depends only on its current value and the values of neighboring pixels.
- **Image transformation**: Operations like rotating, scaling, or flipping images can be performed in parallel by processing different sections or pixels of the image simultaneously.

2. Data Analysis

In **data analysis**, parallel algorithms are used to speed up the processing of large datasets. Common tasks that benefit from parallelism include:

- **Sorting**: Large datasets can be sorted faster using parallel sorting algorithms (e.g., parallel merge sort).
- **Matrix operations**: Operations like matrix multiplication, which are essential in numerical simulations and machine learning, are often parallelized to handle large matrices more efficiently.
- **Machine learning**: Training machine learning models, especially deep learning models, often involves large amounts of data and matrix operations, making them ideal candidates for parallel computing.

Exercise: Implementing Parallel Algorithms Using Python

Let's implement a **parallel algorithm** for sorting a large dataset using **parallel merge sort**. We'll use Python's **concurrent.futures** module to parallelize the merge sort algorithm.

Parallel Merge Sort Algorithm

Merge Sort is a classic divide-and-conquer algorithm that divides the array into two halves, sorts them, and merges them back together. Parallelizing the merge sort involves recursively sorting the subarrays in parallel.

python

```python
import concurrent.futures

# Merge function to combine two sorted halves
def merge(left, right):
    merged = []
    while left and right:
        if left[0] < right[0]:
            merged.append(left.pop(0))
        else:
            merged.append(right.pop(0))
    merged.extend(left)
    merged.extend(right)
    return merged

# Parallel merge sort function
def parallel_merge_sort(arr):
    if len(arr) <= 1:
        return arr

    # Split the array into two halves
```

```
    mid = len(arr) // 2
    left = arr[:mid]
    right = arr[mid:]

    # Use concurrent.futures to parallelize the
sorting of the two halves
    with concurrent.futures.ThreadPoolExecutor()
as executor:
        left_future                            =
executor.submit(parallel_merge_sort, left)
        right_future                           =
executor.submit(parallel_merge_sort, right)

        left_sorted = left_future.result()
        right_sorted = right_future.result()

    # Merge the sorted halves
    return merge(left_sorted, right_sorted)

# Example usage:
arr = [38, 27, 43, 3, 9, 82, 10]
sorted_arr = parallel_merge_sort(arr)
print(f"Sorted array: {sorted_arr}")
```

Explanation:

1. **Merge function**: The merge function takes two sorted lists, left and right, and merges them into a single sorted list.

247

2. **Parallel merge sort**: The `parallel_merge_sort` function splits the input array into two halves, and the sorting of each half is parallelized using Python's `ThreadPoolExecutor`.

3. **ThreadPoolExecutor**: This allows us to run the `parallel_merge_sort` function on both halves of the array in parallel.

Time Complexity: In parallel merge sort, the time complexity for sorting **n** elements is **O(n log n)**, similar to the sequential version. However, the constant factors are significantly reduced with parallelization, especially for large datasets.

Space Complexity: **O(n)**, as we need additional space to store the merged array.

Optimizing Parallel Algorithms

While parallel algorithms can dramatically improve performance, the **speedup** depends on various factors, including:

- **Number of processors or cores**: More cores generally lead to better performance, but after a certain point, additional cores provide diminishing returns.
- **Granularity of tasks**: The size of the tasks being parallelized affects how much overhead is involved in

managing parallelism. Very small tasks may not justify the overhead of parallel execution.

- **Load balancing**: Efficient distribution of tasks across processors ensures that all cores are utilized effectively. Poor load balancing can lead to idle processors and reduce the benefits of parallelism.

A common performance measure for parallel algorithms is **Amdahl's Law**, which describes the theoretical speedup of a parallelized algorithm based on the fraction of the computation that can be parallelized.

Real-World Tools and Libraries for Parallel Computing in Python

Python provides several libraries and frameworks for parallel computing, including:

- `concurrent.futures`: A high-level API for launching parallel tasks using threads or processes.
- `multiprocessing`: A Python module for creating processes, which is useful for CPU-bound tasks (where the Global Interpreter Lock (GIL) can be a limitation).
- `joblib`: A library optimized for parallel processing of loops in numerical computations, often used in machine learning and scientific computing.

- **Dask**: A parallel computing framework that scales from multi-core machines to large clusters and is used for data analysis, machine learning, and more.

Summary of Chapter 23

In this chapter, we introduced **parallel algorithms** and explored their use in speeding up computational tasks by leveraging parallel computing. Key concepts included:

- **Divide-and-conquer** algorithms that can be efficiently parallelized.
- **Real-world applications** of parallel algorithms in **image processing**, **data analysis**, and **machine learning**.
- We implemented a **parallel merge sort** using Python's `concurrent.futures` module to showcase how to parallelize tasks in Python.

Parallel algorithms are a crucial tool for solving large-scale problems, and Python provides various tools to implement them efficiently. As computational tasks become more complex and datasets grow larger, parallel computing will continue to play an increasingly important role in many fields. In the next chapters, we will delve into further optimization techniques and advanced algorithms for high-performance computing.

CHAPTER 24

MACHINE LEARNING ALGORITHMS

Introduction to Machine Learning Algorithms

Machine learning algorithms are designed to allow systems to automatically learn and improve from experience without being explicitly programmed. These algorithms enable computers to recognize patterns, make predictions, and make decisions based on data. Unlike traditional algorithms, which follow a set of predefined rules, machine learning algorithms adapt and adjust their behavior based on the data they process.

In this chapter, we will explore some foundational machine learning algorithms, including:

- **Linear Regression**: A simple model used for predicting continuous variables.
- **Decision Trees**: A model used for classification and regression tasks.
- **K-Means Clustering**: An unsupervised algorithm used for clustering data into groups.

We will also discuss how these algorithms differ from traditional algorithms and provide real-world applications of machine learning.

---

1. Linear Regression

Linear regression is one of the simplest and most widely used machine learning algorithms. It is used for predicting a continuous target variable based on one or more input features. The goal is to find the best-fit line that minimizes the difference between the predicted and actual values of the target variable.

Mathematics of Linear Regression:

In simple linear regression, the relationship between the target variable yyy and the input feature xxx is modeled as:

$$y=\theta 0+\theta 1xy = \theta\_0 + \theta\_1\ xy=\theta 0+\theta 1x$$

Where:

- yyy is the target variable (dependent variable).
- xxx is the input feature (independent variable).
- $\theta 0\theta\_0\theta 0$ is the intercept (bias term).
- $\theta 1\theta\_1\theta 1$ is the coefficient (slope of the line).

The goal of linear regression is to find the values of θ_0\theta_0θ_0 and θ_1\theta_1θ_1 that minimize the **mean squared error (MSE)** between the predicted values and the actual values.

Example: Linear Regression using Python:

python

```python
import numpy as np
import matplotlib.pyplot as plt
from        sklearn.linear_model        import
LinearRegression

# Sample data: hours studied vs. exam scores
X = np.array([[1], [2], [3], [4], [5]])  # Hours
studied
y = np.array([2, 4, 5, 4, 5])  # Exam scores

# Initialize and fit the model
model = LinearRegression()
model.fit(X, y)

# Make predictions
y_pred = model.predict(X)

# Plot the data and the linear regression line
plt.scatter(X, y, color='blue', label='Data
points')
plt.plot(X, y_pred, color='red', label='Fitted
line')
```

```
plt.xlabel('Hours studied')
plt.ylabel('Exam score')
plt.legend()
plt.show()

# Print the model coefficients
print(f"Intercept: {model.intercept_}")
print(f"Slope: {model.coef_}")
```

Explanation:

- We use **scikit-learn**'s LinearRegression class to fit a model to the data and predict the exam scores based on the number of hours studied.
- The plot visualizes the data points and the best-fit line that the algorithm computes.

Time Complexity: **O(n)**, where **n** is the number of data points. This is for the case of simple linear regression.

---

2. Decision Trees

Decision trees are a non-linear model used for both **classification** and **regression** tasks. They work by recursively splitting the data into subsets based on feature values, forming a tree-like structure. Each internal node of the tree represents a decision based on a feature, and each leaf node represents a prediction or a class label.

254

How Decision Trees Work:

- At each node, the algorithm selects the feature that best splits the data into homogeneous groups using a measure such as **Gini impurity** (for classification) or **mean squared error** (for regression).
- The process continues recursively, forming branches, until a stopping condition is met (e.g., a maximum depth or no further improvement in splitting).

Example: Decision Tree using Python (for Classification):

python

```
from sklearn.tree import DecisionTreeClassifier
from sklearn.datasets import load_iris
from        sklearn.model_selection        import
train_test_split
from sklearn import tree

# Load Iris dataset
iris = load_iris()
X = iris.data
y = iris.target

# Split into training and testing sets
X_train,    X_test,    y_train,    y_test    =
train_test_split(X,    y,    test_size=0.3,
random_state=42)
```

```python
# Initialize and train the Decision Tree model
clf = DecisionTreeClassifier(random_state=42)
clf.fit(X_train, y_train)

# Make predictions
y_pred = clf.predict(X_test)

# Print accuracy
accuracy = (y_pred == y_test).mean()
print(f"Accuracy: {accuracy * 100:.2f}%")

# Plot the tree
tree.plot_tree(clf, filled=True)
plt.show()
```

Explanation:

- We use **scikit-learn's** `DecisionTreeClassifier` to train a decision tree on the Iris dataset and then visualize the tree.
- The decision tree is used to classify the species of flowers based on their features (e.g., petal and sepal lengths).

Time Complexity: The time complexity of decision trees depends on the number of nodes and the depth of the tree, generally **O(n log n)** for training.

3. K-Means Clustering

K-Means is an **unsupervised** machine learning algorithm used for clustering. The goal is to partition the data into **k** clusters, where each data point belongs to the cluster with the nearest centroid. The algorithm iterates between two steps:

1. **Assignment step**: Assign each data point to the nearest centroid.
2. **Update step**: Compute the new centroid of each cluster.

The algorithm stops when the centroids no longer change or when a maximum number of iterations is reached.

Example: K-Means Clustering using Python:

python

```
from sklearn.cluster import KMeans
import numpy as np
import matplotlib.pyplot as plt

# Sample data
X = np.array([[1, 2], [1, 4], [1, 0], [4, 2], [4,
4], [4, 0]])

# Apply K-Means with 2 clusters
kmeans = KMeans(n_clusters=2, random_state=42)
kmeans.fit(X)
```

```
# Get the cluster centers and labels
centroids = kmeans.cluster_centers_
labels = kmeans.labels_

# Plot the data points and cluster centers
plt.scatter(X[:,    0],    X[:,    1],    c=labels,
cmap='viridis')
plt.scatter(centroids[:,   0],   centroids[:,   1],
marker='x', color='red')
plt.show()

print(f"Cluster centers: {centroids}")
print(f"Labels: {labels}")
```

Explanation:

- We use **scikit-learn**'s KMeans to cluster a set of 2D data points into 2 clusters.
- The result is plotted, showing the data points colored according to their cluster and the cluster centers marked with a red 'X'.

Time Complexity: The time complexity of K-Means is **O(n * k * i)**, where **n** is the number of data points, **k** is the number of clusters, and **i** is the number of iterations.

How Machine Learning Algorithms Are Similar to Traditional Algorithms

While **machine learning algorithms** and **traditional algorithms** both aim to solve problems, they differ in approach:

- **Traditional algorithms**: Typically follow a predefined set of rules to solve problems and are deterministic in nature. They are well-suited for problems where the solution is known, and the process is clear (e.g., sorting algorithms, searching algorithms).
- **Machine learning algorithms**: Learn patterns from data to make predictions or decisions. They are often used when the problem is too complex for a predefined solution or when the data is too large to manually define all rules.

However, machine learning algorithms still share common principles with traditional algorithms:

- Both rely on mathematical functions (e.g., objective functions, decision boundaries).
- Both involve data processing and optimization (e.g., minimizing errors, maximizing rewards).
- Both aim to find the most efficient solution to a given problem.

Real-World Applications: Predictive Analytics, Recommendation Systems

1. Predictive Analytics

Machine learning algorithms are widely used for **predictive analytics**, where the goal is to make predictions about future events based on historical data. Examples include:

- **Stock price prediction**: Using time-series data to predict future stock prices.
- **Customer behavior prediction**: Predicting whether a customer will buy a product or not based on their past behavior.
- **Weather forecasting**: Predicting future weather conditions based on historical weather data.

2. Recommendation Systems

Machine learning algorithms are at the core of **recommendation systems**, which suggest products, services, or content based on users' preferences and behavior. Examples include:

- **E-commerce**: Recommending products to users based on their past purchases or browsing history.
- **Streaming services**: Recommending movies or songs based on the user's preferences.

- **Social media**: Suggesting friends or posts based on the user's activity.

Exercise: Implementing a Basic Machine Learning Algorithm Using Python

In this exercise, we implemented basic machine learning algorithms like **Linear Regression, Decision Trees**, and **K-Means Clustering** using Python's **scikit-learn** library. These algorithms are foundational to many machine learning applications and are widely used in real-world problems.

We saw how:

- **Linear regression** can be used to model relationships between variables.
- **Decision trees** can be used for classification tasks.
- **K-means clustering** can group similar data points into clusters.

Machine learning algorithms are powerful tools that help solve complex problems, from predictive analytics to recommendation systems. In the next chapters, we will dive deeper into advanced machine learning techniques and explore their applications in more detail.

CHAPTER 25

ALGORITHM OPTIMIZATION TECHNIQUES

Techniques for Optimizing Algorithm Performance

Algorithm optimization is a crucial step in improving the efficiency of an algorithm, especially when dealing with large datasets or real-time systems. Optimization focuses on improving the algorithm's performance in terms of **time complexity** and **space complexity**.

There are several approaches to optimization:

1. **Reducing Time Complexity**: This can be done by choosing more efficient algorithms, optimizing critical loops, reducing redundant calculations, and applying techniques such as **dynamic programming**, **greedy algorithms**, and **divide-and-conquer**.

2. **Reducing Space Complexity**: This involves minimizing the memory used by the algorithm. Techniques such as **in-place algorithms**, **memoization**, and **using data structures efficiently** can help reduce space usage.

3. **Parallelization**: Leveraging parallel processing to break the task into smaller chunks that can be solved concurrently.

4. **Approximation**: In some cases, it may not be feasible to solve a problem exactly, so approximation algorithms are used to provide near-optimal solutions in a more efficient manner.

5. **Avoiding Repeated Computations**: Techniques like **caching** (e.g., memoization) or **dynamic programming** can help avoid recalculating the same values multiple times.

Let's go over a few specific techniques to optimize time and space complexities.

---

1. Optimizing Time Complexity

- **Choose the Right Data Structure**: Different data structures offer different time complexities for operations like searching, inserting, and deleting. For example:
  - Use **hash tables** for fast lookups (average time complexity of $O(1)$).
  - Use **heaps** for efficient minimum or maximum extraction.

- o Use **balanced trees** (e.g., AVL trees, Red-Black trees) for efficient search, insert, and delete operations.
- **Divide-and-Conquer Algorithms**: These algorithms break a problem down into smaller subproblems and solve each one recursively, often improving time complexity:
  - o **Merge Sort** and **QuickSort** are better than bubble sort for large datasets.
- **Dynamic Programming**: In problems with overlapping subproblems, use dynamic programming to store results of subproblems and reuse them. This reduces redundant computations and can convert an exponential time algorithm into a polynomial time one.

  Example: Calculating Fibonacci numbers

  - o Recursive Fibonacci has **O(2^n)** time complexity.
  - o Using dynamic programming or memoization, we can reduce this to **O(n)**.
- **Greedy Algorithms**: Greedy algorithms make locally optimal choices at each step, and while they don't always guarantee the global optimum, they are often faster and simpler to implement. Examples include:
  - o **Huffman coding**
  - o **Dijkstra's shortest path algorithm**

2. Optimizing Space Complexity

- **In-Place Algorithms**: Modify data structures directly rather than creating new ones. This minimizes memory usage. For example:
  - **In-place sorting algorithms** like **QuickSort** and **Insertion Sort** modify the input array directly without requiring additional space.
- **Memoization**: Use memoization to store previously computed results to avoid redundant calculations. This is particularly useful for **recursive algorithms** (e.g., calculating Fibonacci numbers or solving the **Knapsack Problem**).
- **Using Efficient Data Structures**: Choose data structures that minimize memory usage while still providing the functionality required. For example:
  - Use **bit vectors** for representing sets instead of arrays when working with binary data.
  - Use **tries** (prefix trees) for efficiently storing sets of strings in a compact form.
- **Lazy Evaluation**: In cases where you don't need all results immediately, use lazy evaluation to compute values only when needed. This can reduce memory overhead, especially in the case of large datasets.

3. Real-World Application: Optimizing Database Queries, Sorting Large Datasets

Optimizing Database Queries

In databases, optimizing queries is crucial for ensuring fast data retrieval, especially as the database grows in size. Key techniques include:

- **Indexing**: Create indexes on frequently queried columns to speed up lookups. However, be mindful of the space complexity, as indexes can consume significant memory.
- **Query Optimization**: Write efficient SQL queries by using joins effectively and minimizing unnecessary data retrieval. Use **EXPLAIN** to analyze query execution plans.
- **Denormalization**: In some cases, it may be more efficient to duplicate data across tables to reduce the number of joins needed.

Optimizing Sorting Large Datasets

Sorting large datasets efficiently requires using algorithms that minimize both time and space complexities:

- **External Sorting**: When the data is too large to fit into memory, use external sorting techniques, which involve sorting the data in chunks that fit in memory and then merging the results.

- **Parallel Sorting**: For very large datasets, parallelizing the sorting process can reduce runtime. You can break the dataset into smaller chunks, sort them in parallel, and then merge the sorted chunks.

Exercise: Optimizing a Given Algorithm for Time and Space Efficiency

Let's optimize a basic algorithm—**Bubble Sort**—for both time and space efficiency.

Bubble Sort (inefficient):

Bubble sort repeatedly compares adjacent elements and swaps them if they are in the wrong order. It's a simple algorithm but has a time complexity of **$O(n^2)$**, making it inefficient for large datasets.

python

```python
def bubble_sort(arr):
    n = len(arr)
    for i in range(n):
        for j in range(0, n-i-1):
            if arr[j] > arr[j+1]:
```

```
            arr[j],  arr[j+1]  =  arr[j+1],
arr[j]
    return arr
```

```
# Example usage:
arr = [64, 34, 25, 12, 22, 11, 90]
print("Sorted array:", bubble_sort(arr))
```

Time Complexity: O(n²)

Optimized Bubble Sort (with early termination):

We can optimize bubble sort by introducing an early termination. If during a pass no swaps are made, the array is already sorted, and we can stop early.

python

```
def optimized_bubble_sort(arr):
    n = len(arr)
    for i in range(n):
        swapped = False   # Flag to check if a
swap has occurred
        for j in range(0, n-i-1):
            if arr[j] > arr[j+1]:
                arr[j],  arr[j+1]  =  arr[j+1],
arr[j]
                swapped = True
        if not swapped:
```

```
            break  # If no swaps occurred, array
is sorted
    return arr


# Example usage:
arr = [64, 34, 25, 12, 22, 11, 90]
print("Sorted                          array:",
optimized_bubble_sort(arr))
```

Time Complexity: **O(n²)** in the worst case, but **O(n)** if the array is already sorted. **Space Complexity**: **O(1)**, as the algorithm sorts in-place without needing extra space.

Optimizing with Merge Sort (Time and Space Efficiency)

Now, let's implement a more efficient algorithm like **Merge Sort** to demonstrate how a more efficient algorithm can optimize performance.

python

```
def merge_sort(arr):
    if len(arr) <= 1:
        return arr
    mid = len(arr) // 2
    left = merge_sort(arr[:mid])
    right = merge_sort(arr[mid:])
```

```
        return merge(left, right)

def merge(left, right):
    sorted_arr = []
    while left and right:
        if left[0] < right[0]:
            sorted_arr.append(left.pop(0))
        else:
            sorted_arr.append(right.pop(0))
    sorted_arr.extend(left)
    sorted_arr.extend(right)
    return sorted_arr

# Example usage:
arr = [64, 34, 25, 12, 22, 11, 90]
print("Sorted array:", merge_sort(arr))
```

Time Complexity: **O(n log n)**, which is much more efficient than bubble sort for large datasets. **Space Complexity**: **O(n)**, as additional space is needed for storing the left and right subarrays.

Summary of Chapter 25

In this chapter, we explored **algorithm optimization techniques** focused on improving both **time complexity** and **space complexity**. We discussed various methods to enhance performance, such as:

- **Reducing time complexity** by using efficient algorithms (e.g., merge sort instead of bubble sort).
- **Reducing space complexity** using in-place algorithms and memoization.
- **Real-world applications** of optimization, including database query optimization and sorting large datasets.

Through the exercise of optimizing **Bubble Sort** into **Optimized Bubble Sort** and using **Merge Sort**, we demonstrated how to make algorithms more efficient in terms of both time and space. Optimizing algorithms is a critical skill in solving large-scale problems in computer science and software development. In the next chapters, we will explore further advanced topics in optimization and computational efficiency.

CHAPTER 26

DEBUGGING AND TESTING ALGORITHMS

Tools and Techniques for Debugging and Testing Algorithms

Debugging and **testing** are crucial aspects of software development, especially when working with complex algorithms. They ensure that algorithms function as intended and produce correct, efficient results.

In this chapter, we will cover tools and techniques for debugging and testing algorithms, including:

- **Common debugging strategies** and tools.
- **Unit testing** frameworks.
- **Validating algorithm correctness** with test cases.

---

1. Debugging Algorithms

Debugging is the process of identifying and fixing errors (or "bugs") in a program or algorithm. There are various types of errors, including:

- **Syntax errors**: Mistakes in the structure of the code.

272

- **Logical errors**: Errors that occur when the code runs without crashing, but the algorithm does not produce the expected result.

- **Runtime errors**: Errors that occur during the execution of the program, such as division by zero or accessing out-of-bounds array indices.

Common Debugging Strategies:

1. **Print Statements**: Use print statements at key points in the algorithm to inspect variable values and understand how the algorithm progresses.

2. **Interactive Debuggers**: Tools like **Python's pdb** or **IDE-based debuggers** allow you to set breakpoints, step through the code line by line, and inspect the state of variables at runtime.

3. **Code Reviews**: Often, reviewing code with peers can help identify potential issues that you may have overlooked.

4. **Unit Tests**: Writing tests for individual functions and algorithms can help identify and fix bugs early in the development process.

Tools for Debugging:

- **Python Debugger (pdb)**: Python's built-in debugger allows you to pause execution, inspect variables, and step through the code interactively.
  - ○ Example: Add `import pdb;` `pdb.set_trace()` at the point where you want to pause execution.
- **IDE Debuggers**: Most integrated development environments (IDEs) like **PyCharm**, **VSCode**, or **Eclipse** have built-in debuggers that allow for easy stepping through code and variable inspection.

---

2. Writing Unit Tests to Validate the Correctness of Algorithms

Unit testing involves writing tests for individual components or functions of the program. Unit tests are typically small and focus on validating the behavior of a specific algorithm or function, ensuring it behaves as expected.

Benefits of Unit Testing:

- **Correctness**: Verifies that the algorithm produces the correct output for a given input.

- **Refactoring Safety**: Helps ensure that changes or optimizations to the algorithm do not break existing functionality.
- **Regression Detection**: Detects when an algorithm behaves incorrectly due to new changes in the code.

Unit Testing Frameworks:

- **Python's `unittest`**: A built-in module that allows you to define test cases and run them automatically.
- **`pytest`**: A third-party framework that is more flexible and user-friendly, particularly for writing and running tests.

Writing Unit Tests:

1. **Test Inputs**: Write test cases for various input types, including typical inputs, edge cases, and invalid inputs.
2. **Expected Outputs**: Define what the expected output should be for each test case.
3. **Assertions**: Use assertions to compare the actual output of the algorithm with the expected output.

Example: Unit testing a sorting algorithm using `unittest`:

python

```
import unittest
```

```python
# Example: Bubble Sort Function
def bubble_sort(arr):
    n = len(arr)
    for i in range(n):
        for j in range(0, n-i-1):
            if arr[j] > arr[j+1]:
                arr[j], arr[j+1] = arr[j+1],
arr[j]
    return arr


# Unit test for bubble_sort
class TestSortingAlgorithms(unittest.TestCase):

    def test_bubble_sort(self):
        # Test typical case
        self.assertEqual(bubble_sort([3, 1, 4,
1, 5, 9, 2, 6, 5]), [1, 1, 2, 3, 4, 5, 5, 6, 9])

        # Test already sorted array
        self.assertEqual(bubble_sort([1, 2, 3,
4, 5]), [1, 2, 3, 4, 5])

        # Test empty array
        self.assertEqual(bubble_sort([]), [])

        # Test array with one element
        self.assertEqual(bubble_sort([42]),
[42])
```

```
# Test reverse sorted array
self.assertEqual(bubble_sort([5,  4,  3,
2, 1]), [1, 2, 3, 4, 5])

if __name__ == '__main__':
    unittest.main()
```

Explanation:

- We define a simple **bubble sort** function and create a test class `TestSortingAlgorithms` to test it.
- Each test case uses `assertEqual` to compare the actual output of the algorithm with the expected output.

Time Complexity of Unit Testing:

- **Test Case Execution**: The time complexity of each unit test depends on the algorithm being tested. For example, testing **bubble sort** with a large input will have a time complexity of **O(n²)** for each test case.

---

3. Real-World Example: Validating Sorting and Search Algorithms

Let's explore how to validate common algorithms such as **sorting** and **searching** with unit tests.

Validating a Sorting Algorithm:

For a sorting algorithm (like bubble sort or merge sort), we typically check:

- **Correctness**: The output should be sorted in non-decreasing order.
- **Edge Cases**: The algorithm should handle edge cases, such as empty arrays, arrays with one element, or arrays with identical elements.
- **Performance**: For large inputs, the algorithm should run within a reasonable time limit (though this is more of an integration test than a unit test).

Validating a Search Algorithm:

For a search algorithm (like binary search), we test:

- **Correctness**: The search should return the correct index for an existing element or -1 for a non-existent element.
- **Edge Cases**: Search on empty arrays, arrays with one element, or unsorted arrays (if the algorithm requires sorted input).
- **Boundary Conditions**: Test for searching at the beginning and end of the array.

Example: Unit testing a binary search algorithm:

python

```python
def binary_search(arr, target):
    low, high = 0, len(arr) - 1
    while low <= high:
        mid = (low + high) // 2
        if arr[mid] == target:
            return mid
        elif arr[mid] < target:
            low = mid + 1
        else:
            high = mid - 1
    return -1

# Unit test for binary_search
class TestSearchAlgorithms(unittest.TestCase):

    def test_binary_search(self):
        arr = [1, 2, 3, 4, 5, 6, 7, 8, 9]

        # Test for a present element
        self.assertEqual(binary_search(arr,  4),
3)

        # Test for a non-present element
        self.assertEqual(binary_search(arr, 10),
-1)

        # Test for an element at the start
```

```
        self.assertEqual(binary_search(arr,   1),
0)


        # Test for an element at the end
        self.assertEqual(binary_search(arr,   9),
8)


        # Test on empty array
        self.assertEqual(binary_search([], 3), -
1)


if __name__ == '__main__':
    unittest.main()
```

Explanation:

- This unit test verifies the **binary search** function by checking if the target element is found at the correct index or if -1 is returned when the element is not present.

---

4. Exercise: Writing Test Cases for an Algorithm

Let's write test cases for a **merge sort** algorithm. The goal is to ensure that the algorithm works correctly under various conditions.

Merge Sort Algorithm:

python

```python
def merge_sort(arr):
    if len(arr) <= 1:
        return arr
    mid = len(arr) // 2
    left = merge_sort(arr[:mid])
    right = merge_sort(arr[mid:])

    return merge(left, right)

def merge(left, right):
    sorted_arr = []
    while left and right:
        if left[0] < right[0]:
            sorted_arr.append(left.pop(0))
        else:
            sorted_arr.append(right.pop(0))
    sorted_arr.extend(left)
    sorted_arr.extend(right)
    return sorted_arr

# Unit test for merge_sort
class TestSortingAlgorithms(unittest.TestCase):

    def test_merge_sort(self):
        # Test typical case
        self.assertEqual(merge_sort([38, 27, 43,
3, 9, 82, 10]), [3, 9, 10, 27, 38, 43, 82])
```

```
        # Test already sorted array
        self.assertEqual(merge_sort([1, 2, 3, 4,
5]), [1, 2, 3, 4, 5])

        # Test empty array
        self.assertEqual(merge_sort([]), [])

        # Test array with one element
        self.assertEqual(merge_sort([42]), [42])

        # Test reverse sorted array
        self.assertEqual(merge_sort([5, 4, 3, 2,
1]), [1, 2, 3, 4, 5])

if __name__ == '__main__':
    unittest.main()
```

Explanation:

- The **merge sort** algorithm is tested on various types of input: typical unsorted arrays, already sorted arrays, empty arrays, and arrays with one element.
- Each test case verifies that the function produces the correct output and handles edge cases.

Summary of Chapter 26

In this chapter, we learned about **debugging** and **testing algorithms** to ensure they perform correctly and efficiently:

- **Debugging** tools like print statements, interactive debuggers (e.g., `pdb`), and IDE debuggers help identify and fix issues in algorithms.
- **Unit testing** frameworks such as `unittest` and `pytest` help validate the correctness of algorithms by defining and running test cases.
- We wrote unit tests for sorting algorithms (e.g., **Bubble Sort** and **Merge Sort**) and search algorithms (e.g., **Binary Search**), ensuring that they perform correctly under different conditions.

By incorporating debugging and testing into the development process, we ensure that our algorithms are robust, reliable, and efficient, and that they continue to work as expected even when modified or optimized.

CHAPTER 27

REAL-WORLD USE CASES AND APPLICATIONS

How Algorithms Are Applied in Real-World Scenarios Across Industries

Algorithms are at the heart of modern technology and have wide-ranging applications across different industries. In the real world, algorithms help solve complex problems, automate tasks, improve decision-making, and optimize processes. The use of algorithms has become essential in diverse domains, from e-commerce platforms to healthcare and autonomous vehicles.

In this chapter, we will explore how algorithms are applied in real-world scenarios across various industries, highlight some case studies, and discuss future trends in algorithm development.

---

1. Case Studies: E-commerce Platforms, Healthcare, Autonomous Vehicles

E-commerce Platforms

In **e-commerce**, algorithms play a central role in personalizing user experiences, optimizing supply chains, and improving business decision-making. Key algorithms used in e-commerce include:

- **Recommendation Systems**: E-commerce platforms like Amazon, eBay, and Netflix use recommendation algorithms to suggest products or content based on user preferences, past behavior, and interactions. These algorithms can use **collaborative filtering**, **content-based filtering**, or a hybrid approach to provide personalized recommendations.

  o **Example**: Amazon's recommendation engine uses collaborative filtering to suggest products by analyzing user activity and the purchases of other users with similar interests.

- **Dynamic Pricing Algorithms**: E-commerce platforms also use pricing algorithms that adjust prices based on demand, competition, time of day, or customer profiles. These dynamic pricing models can maximize revenue, attract more customers, and clear inventory.

- **Search and Sorting Algorithms**: Algorithms such as **binary search** and **quick sort** are used to efficiently search for products and display results based on relevance, price, popularity, etc.

Healthcare

In **healthcare**, algorithms are transforming patient care, diagnostics, and operations. Some applications of algorithms in healthcare include:

- **Predictive Analytics**: Healthcare providers use machine learning algorithms to predict patient outcomes, such as the likelihood of developing a chronic disease or the probability of hospital readmission. These predictions help in early intervention and personalized treatment plans.
  - o **Example**: Hospitals use algorithms to predict patient outcomes based on medical history, lab results, and other factors. These predictions help physicians provide timely treatment to high-risk patients.
- **Medical Imaging and Diagnosis**: **Image processing algorithms** are used to analyze medical images, such as X-rays, MRIs, and CT scans, to detect abnormalities such as tumors, fractures, and diseases. **Convolutional Neural Networks (CNNs)**, a type of deep learning algorithm, are particularly effective for this purpose.
  - o **Example**: AI-driven systems, such as IBM Watson Health, use deep learning algorithms to analyze medical images and assist doctors in

diagnosing diseases like cancer more accurately and faster than human clinicians.

- **Drug Discovery and Development**: Algorithms are used in bioinformatics and pharmacology to analyze complex biological data, model molecular structures, and identify potential drug candidates. **Genetic algorithms** and **neural networks** are employed to optimize the process of drug discovery.

Autonomous Vehicles

The development of **autonomous vehicles** has become one of the most significant applications of algorithms in recent years. Key algorithms used in autonomous vehicles include:

- **Path Planning and Navigation Algorithms**: These algorithms allow autonomous vehicles to navigate safely through complex environments. Algorithms like *A search**, **Dijkstra's algorithm**, and **RRT (Rapidly-exploring Random Trees)** are used to find optimal or feasible paths while avoiding obstacles.
  - o **Example**: Tesla's Autopilot uses algorithms to continuously calculate the safest and most efficient route while adjusting to real-time traffic conditions and road hazards.
- **Object Detection and Recognition**: Computer vision algorithms help autonomous vehicles detect and

recognize objects, pedestrians, and other vehicles on the road. **Convolutional Neural Networks (CNNs)** are widely used for real-time object detection and classification.

- o **Example**: Waymo, a leader in self-driving technology, uses deep learning-based algorithms to process data from sensors and cameras to detect objects like traffic lights, pedestrians, and road signs.

- **Sensor Fusion Algorithms**: Autonomous vehicles rely on data from multiple sensors, including cameras, radar, and LiDAR. Sensor fusion algorithms combine these inputs to create a comprehensive understanding of the vehicle's surroundings.

  - o **Example**: Waymo's vehicles use sensor fusion algorithms to integrate inputs from LiDAR and cameras to create detailed 3D maps of the environment and make real-time decisions.

---

2. Discussion on Future Trends in Algorithm Development

As technology continues to evolve, so do the algorithms that power it. Here are some future trends in algorithm development:

- **Quantum Computing Algorithms**: With the rise of quantum computing, algorithms are being developed to leverage quantum mechanics for solving problems that are currently intractable for classical computers. Quantum algorithms, like **Shor's algorithm** for factoring large numbers and **Grover's algorithm** for searching unsorted databases, could revolutionize fields such as cryptography and optimization.

- **Artificial General Intelligence (AGI)**: While **narrow AI** algorithms excel in specific tasks, researchers are working towards **AGI**—algorithms that can learn and perform any intellectual task that humans can do. Achieving AGI would require breakthroughs in reinforcement learning, natural language processing, and multi-task learning.

- **Explainable AI (XAI)**: As machine learning models become more complex, there is a growing need for algorithms that can explain how decisions are made, especially in sensitive fields like healthcare and finance. **Explainable AI** aims to make AI systems more transparent and interpretable, which will foster trust and broader adoption.

- **Federated Learning**: This is a new paradigm in machine learning where multiple devices or nodes collaboratively train a model without sharing raw data. Federated learning enables privacy-preserving algorithms, which is crucial in industries like healthcare and finance, where data privacy is paramount.

- **Edge Computing and Algorithms**: Edge computing brings computation closer to the data source (such as IoT devices) rather than relying on centralized data centers. Algorithms designed for **edge computing** will need to be optimized for low-latency, low-bandwidth environments, making them more efficient for real-time processing.

- **Ethical and Fair Algorithms**: As algorithms make decisions that affect people's lives, such as hiring, lending, or criminal sentencing, ensuring that these algorithms are ethical and fair is becoming a priority. Future algorithm development will include measures to mitigate biases and ensure fairness in decision-making.

---

3. Conclusion and Next Steps: How to Continue Mastering Algorithms

Mastering algorithms is a continuous journey. While this book has provided a foundation for understanding the principles, techniques, and applications of algorithms, the field is vast and constantly evolving. Here are some next steps you can take to continue your journey in mastering algorithms:

1. **Practice, Practice, Practice**: Consistently solving algorithmic problems on platforms like **LeetCode**, **HackerRank**, and **CodeSignal** will improve your

problem-solving skills and deepen your understanding of algorithmic concepts.

2. **Explore Advanced Topics**: Dive deeper into advanced algorithms such as **graph algorithms**, **dynamic programming**, **greedy algorithms**, **string matching algorithms**, and **computational geometry**.

3. **Contribute to Open Source**: Contribute to open-source projects that involve complex algorithms. Working on real-world projects will help you understand how algorithms are applied in practice and provide invaluable experience.

4. **Stay Updated with Research**: Algorithms are an active area of research. Keeping up with academic papers, blogs, and conferences such as **NeurIPS**, **ICML**, and **CVPR** will expose you to the latest trends and innovations in algorithm development.

5. **Work on Real-World Problems**: Start building real-world applications that leverage algorithms. Whether it's creating a recommendation system for a website, implementing search algorithms for a large dataset, or working on AI-powered applications, applying algorithms to solve practical problems will reinforce your learning.

6. **Learn About Data Structures**: Algorithms and data structures go hand-in-hand. Understanding the right data structure for a given problem is essential to creating

efficient algorithms. Consider studying **trees, graphs, heaps, hash tables**, and **trie structures**.

7. **Collaboration and Networking**: Join algorithm-focused communities or attend conferences where you can collaborate with like-minded individuals, exchange ideas, and stay motivated.

Summary of Chapter 27

In this chapter, we explored the real-world applications of algorithms in industries such as **e-commerce, healthcare**, and **autonomous vehicles**. These case studies demonstrated how algorithms solve complex, large-scale problems in a wide variety of domains. We also discussed future trends in algorithm development, such as **quantum computing, artificial general intelligence, federated learning**, and **explainable AI**.

Finally, we outlined actionable steps for continuing your journey in mastering algorithms. By practicing regularly, exploring advanced topics, contributing to open-source projects, and staying updated with research, you can continue to grow your skills and apply algorithms to real-world challenges.

As the world becomes increasingly data-driven, the ability to design, analyze, and apply efficient algorithms will remain a valuable and in-demand skill. Keep learning, experimenting, and solving problems to advance your understanding and mastery of algorithms.